S0-GQE-001

LAKE COUNTRY
COOKBOOK

by

Bruce Carlson

© 1993 by Bruce Carlson

All rights reserved. No part of this book may be reproduced or transmitted in any form or by any means, electronic or mechanical, including photocopying, recording or by any informational storage or retrieval system, except by a reviewer who may quote brief passages in a review to be printed in a magazine or newspaper-without permission in writing from the publisher. For information contact Bruce Carlson, Quixote Press, R.R. #4, Box 33B, Blvd. Station, Sioux City, Iowa 51109.

* * * * * * * * * *

**QUIXOTE
PRESS**
Bruce Carlson
R.R. #4, Box 33B
Blvd. Station
Sioux City, Iowa
51109

PRINTED
IN
U.S.A.

iii

DEDICATION

-to our local ladies (and gents) who can turn a fish into a feast.

TABLE OF CONTENTS

ACKNOWLEDGEMENTS

I sure want to recognize the many good cooks, find cooks, and excellent cooks who shared their family recipes with me.

B. Carlson

PREFACE

Cooking here in the lakes country is a little bit different than cooking everyplace else in the Midwest. It often uses things from the lakes and from the lowlands near the lakes.

And, it's always good . . . . . . real good.

INTRODUCTION

This book of Lakes Country Cooking is similar to some other cookbooks, but the lakes nearby make themselves felt in the recipes and in that special feeling here among our "mirrors of the sky."

Jan Elwood,
(Nutritionist)

APPETIZERS

and

BEVERAGES

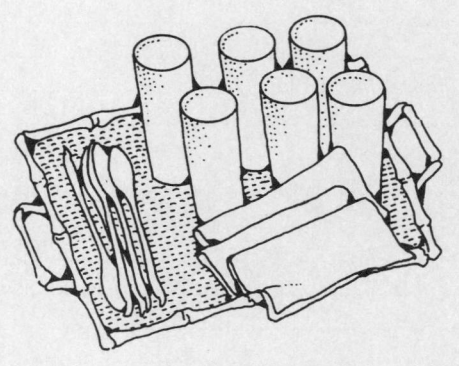

Appetizers and Beverages

Party Mix With Crispix

3 T. butter
1 tsp. seasoned salt
2 tsp. lemon juice
4 tsp. Worcestershire sauce

6 C. Crispix cereal
1 C. pretzels
1 C. salted mixed nuts

Melt butter in 9 x 13-inch pan in 250° oven. Remove and add salt, lemon juice and Worcestershire sauce. Add cereal, pretzels and nuts, stirring until coated. Bake at 250° oven for 45 minutes, stirring every 15 minutes. Spread on paper towels until cool.

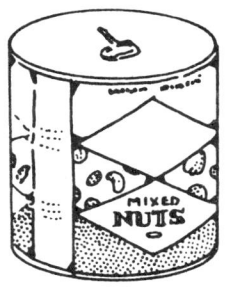

Caramel Corn

2 C. brown sugar
½ C. white syrup
½ tsp. soda

2 sticks margarine (1 C.)
1 tsp. salt
8 qts. popped corn

Combine sugar, margarine, syrup and salt. Boil 5 minutes. Stir in soda after you shut off burner. Stir fast and mix soda in good. Pour over corn and mix well. Put on cookie sheet and place in oven for 1 hour at 250°. Stir about every 15 minutes.

Grape Juice

1 C. purple (Concord) grapes   *1 C. sugar*
Boiling water

Put 1 C. grapes and 1 C. sugar in sterlized quart jar. Fill jar with boiling water and seal immediately. Let set for about 6 weeks. Makes 1 quart delicious grape juice.

Slush

6 oz. lemonade (frozen)   *6 oz. orange juice (frozen)*
6 oz. pineapple juice (frozen)   *2 C. vodka*

Boil 2 C. sugar and 7 C. water. Add frozen juices, mix and freeze. Fill glasses ½ and ½ 7-Up.

Frozen Pineapple Slush

1 (24 oz.) can unsweetened   *1 C. orange juice*
   pineapple juice   *1/8 C. lemon juice*
2 C. water   *2 qts. ginger ale*
1 C. sugar

Bring water and sugar to a boil, then add the juices. Freeze for 12-24 hours. When ready to serve, put some of the slush in a glass and pour ginger ale over it.

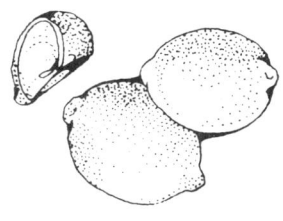

Surf's-Up-Punch

4 cans frozen Hawaiian Punch
11 C. water

1 qt. 7-Up
1 small bottle Ocean Spray
   cranberry juice

Mix together.

Golden Punch

1 (No. 5) apricot nectar
1 (No. 5) gold Hawaiian punch
1 (No. 5) pineapple juice

1 (6 oz.) can frozen orange juice
2 bottles ginger ale

Mix all together, adding ginger ale just before serving.

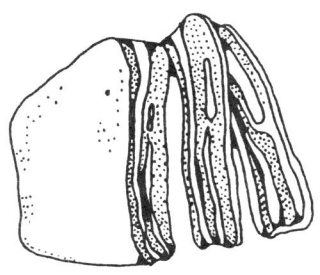

Quiche

3 eggs
½ C. Bisquick
½ C. melted butter
1½ C. milk

¼ tsp. salt
½ C. grated Swiss cheese
½ C. ham or bacon in small
   pieces

Sprinkle over mixture and press to surface with back of spoon. Bake at 350°
for 45 minutes.

Society Chips

14 dill size cucumbers	1 tsp. salt (not iodized)
8 C. sugar	2 T. mixed pickling spices
1 qt. vinegar	(tied in a bag)

Wash cucumbers well and pack in an enamel pan. Cover with boiling water. Pour this off each morning for 3 days and cover with fresh boiling water. On the fourth morning, slice the cucumbers into very thin slices and put back into the cleaned enamel pan. Combine sugar, vinegar, salt and mixed pickling spices. Boil hard. Pour hot syrup over sliced cucumbers. Each morning for three days pour off the syrup. Bring to boil and put back on the cucumbers. On the 4th day bring cucumbers and syrup to boil and put into hot serilized jar. Wipe jar lips well and seal.

Mom's Goodies

1 angel food cake mix	1 C. boiling water
1 bottle strawberry pop	1 pkg. frozen strawberries
2 egg whites	Dream Whip
1 (3 oz.) pkg. strawberry Jello	

Prepare cake mix as directed using pop for liquid. Add egg whites and bake as directed. While cake is cooling, dissovle Jello in water. Cool and add frozen strawberries. When it starts to thicken, fold in 1 C. whipped Dream Whip. Cut cake in 3 equal layers. Put first layer in pan. Clover with half of strawberry mixture. Follow up with second layer and mixture, then third layer. Put in refrigerator until gelatin is thoroughly set. Remove from pan and frost with Dream Whip.

Ritz Goodies

1 lb. box Ritz crackers
1 can sweetened condensed milk

1½ C. finely cut dates
½ C. chopped nutmeats (opt.)

Cook milk and dates until thick, stir constantly. Remove from heat and add nuts. Put a teaspoonful of mixture on each cracker and bake at 350° for 5-8 minutes. Frost with the following frosting and decorate with colored sugar if you desire. Cookies can be frozen.

For Frosting: Mix ¼ C. butter or margarine. 3 oz. pkg. cream cheese, 1 tsp. vanilla and 1¼ C powdered sugar. Beat well.

Cheese Surprise

8 oz. cottage cheese
1 C. soft butter
2 C. flour

¼ stick melted butter or margarine
¾ C. chopped walnuts
¾ C. brown sugar

Blend cheese and butter. Mix in flour to form dough. Roll out into 3 sections as for pie crust. Sprinkle with nuts and brown sugar. Roll as is or cut into pre-shaped wedges. Bake at 375° for 15-20 minutes on greased and floured cookie sheet. Sprinkle with powdered sugar.

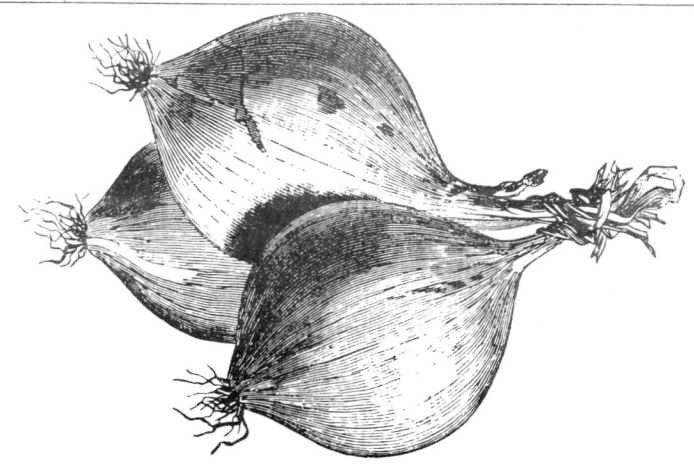

BBQ Beef Cups

¾ lb. ground beef
½ C. barbeque sauce
1 T. instant minced onion

1 can refrigerated biscuits
Salt and pepper
¼ C. shredded cheese

Bake in muffin tins at 400° for 10-15 minutes. Sprinkle with ¼ C. shredded cheese. Return to oven to melt. Makes 10 beef cups.

Cornmeal Balls

½ C. cornmeal
2 tsp. salt
2 C. milk
¾ C. sugar
¾ C. shortening

2 eggs (beaten)
2 pkgs. yeast
1 C. warm water
5-6 C. flour

Cook cornmeal, salt and milk until thick. While still hot add the sugar and shortening; cool. Dissolve yeast in warm water and mix well with cornmeal mixture. Add eggs and stir. Stir in 5 to 6 cups of flour to make medium dough. Knead, put in greased bowl and let rise for about an hour. Divide dough into 6 equal parts. Roll each part into a circle. Brush with melted butter. Cut into 8 pieces pie wedges Start at large end to roll up and place on greased pan. Let rise for about 45 minutes. Bake at 350° for 12-15 minute or until lightly browned.

Fruit Slush

1 (No. 5) can pineapple juice
5 C. water
4 C. sugar
5 bananas (mashed)

1 (6 oz.) can frozen lemonade
2 (6 oz. ea.) cans frozen orange
   juice

Combine pineapple juice, 5 C. water and 4 C. sugar until sugar dissolves. Add lemonade, orange juice and bananas. Mix well and pour into covered container and freeze at least 24 hours. It never freezes hard. To serve: Spoon into glasses and fill with 7-Up or serve over ice cream or add fresh or canned fruits or serve "as is" in sherbet glasses.

Orange Wave

⅓ C. orange juice/Kool Aid/ or
   orange pop

4 heaping scoops vanilla ice cream

Place ingredients in bowl or blender. Mix until smooth. Place in cups and eat with spoon. Makes about 3 or 4 C.

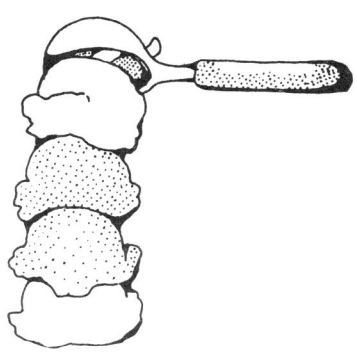

Hot Punch

9 C. cranberry juice
9 C. pineapple juice
4½ C. water
1 C. brown sugar

4 tsp. whole cloves
4 cinnamon sticks
¼ tsp. salt

Put first 4 ingredients into a 30 C. coffee pot. Place cloves, cinnamon sticks and salt in the basket. Brew and serve.

Punch In Green

1 can Hi-C citrus cooler
1 (67 oz. bottle) Ginger ale or 7-Up
1 pkg. lemon-lime Kool-Aid

1 small can frozen lemonade
1 C. sugar
1 Hi-C can of water

Mix all above ingredients together. (Empty the citrus cooler from can and fill can with water for amount of water needed.)

Punch In Blue

4 qts. water
½ C. sugar
11 (6 oz. ea.) can frozen lemonade

11 (12 oz. ea.) bottles 7-Up
1 T. blue food coloring

Mix all ingredients together, except 7-Up. Take out 1 cupfull and add blue coloring to it. Just before serving, add 7-Up and blue color mixture, a little at a time, until you have the shade of blue you want. You may add ½ gallon lemon sherbet too, just before serving. Be sure to use 7-Up if you want true blue.

Good Times Punch

*4 medium grapefruit
  (peeled and cut up)
1 liter bottle lemon-lime beverage*

*¼ C sugar
1 pint lime sherbet and 1 pint
  pineapple sherbet or both
  sherbets of your choice*

In a blender container or food processor bowl, place half of cut-up grapefruit. Cover and blend or process nearly smooth, strain into a large bowl, discard pulp. Repeat with remaining grapefruit. Add half of lemon-lime beverage (4 C.) to grapefruit juice. Stir in sugar until nearly dissolved. Pour into a 9 × 9 × 2-inch pan. Cover and freeze 4-5 hours or until nearly firm, stirring 3 times. At serving time, spoon sherbet into punch bowl. Spoon grapefruit mixture into punch bowl and remaining lemon-lime beverage. Serve immediately. Makes 1 gallon punch.

Cinnamon Cider

1 gallon apple cider

1 C. red hots (imperials candy)

Heat cider on stove in 30-cup coffee server. When hot, stir in the candy and it will dissolve quickly. Adds a pretty pink color to the cider and a mild cinnamon flavor.

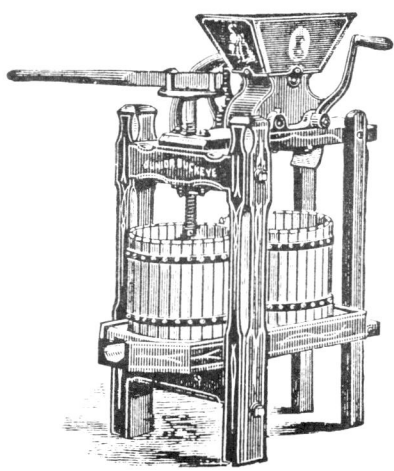

Apple-Cherry Drink

2 pkgs. cherry Kool-Aid
½ C. sugar
1 (6 oz.) can frozen lemonade

1½ qt. apple juice
2¼ qt. ice water

Mix and serve cold. Makes 1 gallon.

Russian Tea

10 oz. Tang
¾ C. instant tea

¾ C. sugar
1 tsp. cinnamon

Mix well and use 2 tsp. in cup of boiling water.

Hot Spiced Pineapple Juice

4 C. pineapple juice
4 C. water
2 sticks cinnamon

1 tsp. whole cloves
1 tsp. whole allspice
¾ C. brown sugar

Put spices in percolator basket. Fill container with juice and water; perk.

Cheese Frenchees

6 slices bread
6 slices American cheese
Mayonnaise or salad dressing
1 egg

½ C. milk
1 tsp. salt
¾ C. flour
Crushed corn flakes

Makes 3 cheese sandwiches of bread and cheese (2 slices in each) and salad dressing. Cut into quarters, combine egg, milk, salt and flour into a smooth batter. Dip each quarter into batter, then into corn flakes. Deep fat until golden brown, 375°. (12 pieces.)

Bohemian Snack Potatoes

4-6 C. potato peelings
½ C. butter

½-1 T. garlic salt
1 T. minced onion

DIP:
1 C. sour cream
¼ C. crumbled blue cheese

½ tsp. minced onion
¼ tsp. seasoned salt

Peel potato rather thick, use insides later. Keep the peel. Place in cold water, refrigerate until ready to use. then pat dry on towel. Melt butter on cookie sheet, spread on peels and seasoning. Bake until brown and crunchy at 375° fr 20-30 minutes. Serve hot with dip.

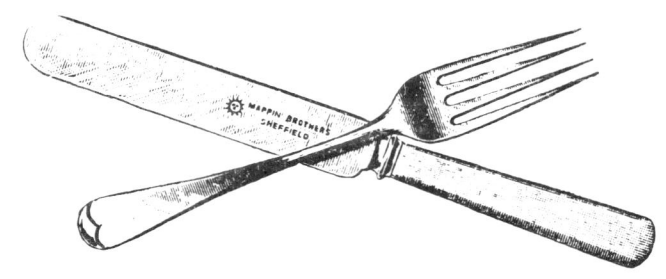

Cheese Log

1 lb. Velveeta cheese
2 (6 oz. ea.) pkgs. Philadelphia
  cream cheese

½ of one onion
Dash of garlic powder
Chopped nuts

Chop the ½ of onion very fine. Mix the Velveeta cheese, Philadelphia cream cheese, chopped half onion and garlic powder. Roll into a log, chill and roll in chopped nuts.

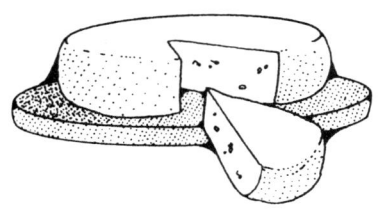

Spinach Balls

2 (10 oz. ea.) pkgs. frozen spinach
  (cooked and well drained)
2 .C packaged stuffing mix
1 C. Parmesan cheese

6 beaten eggs
¾ C. softened oleo
Salt and pepper to taste

Combine all ingredients and mix well. Roll into balls and freeze. Before serving, place on cookie sheet, lightly greased and bake 12-15 minutes at 350°.

Cheese Ball

8 oz. cream cheese (room temp.)
8 oz. cheddar cheese (grated)
¼ C. oleo or butter
1 tsp. Worcestershire sauce

1 tsp. dry mustard
1 tsp. grated onion
Pecan nuts

Mix the cream cheese, grated cheddar and oleo (or butter) together. Add the Worcestershire sauce, dry mustard and grated onion. Roll cheese ball into chopped pecan nuts.

Chili Cheese Log

1 (13¼ oz.) pkg. Cracker Barrel
   cheese (extra sharp)
2 T. lemon juice
8 oz. cream cheese
Garlic salt (as desired)

Dash of salt
Dash of pepper (red)
¼ C. pecans
Paprika
Chili powder

Have cheese at room temperature. Put under MixMaster all of Cracker Barrel cheese, lemon juice, cream cheese and blend well. Add garlic salt (amount varies with taste), salt and pepper. On a piecef waxed paper crush pecans, sprinkle with paprika and chili powder. Roll a 6-inch roll of cheese in the nut and chili mixture. Do same with the rest of cheese mixture. Chill until firm and serve in slices on crisp crackers.

Appetizer With Knorr's

2 pkgs. crescent rolls
1 (8 oz.) pkg. cream cheese

1 C. mayonnaise
1 pkg. Knorr's vegetable soup mix

Press crescent rolls into bottom of 11 x 15-inch pan and bake according to package directions. Cool. Mix remaining ingredients and spread over rolls. Put fresh vegetables on top - green onions, green peppers, radishes, carrots, broccoli, cauliflower. Cut in small squares.

"Just For Notes"

SALADS

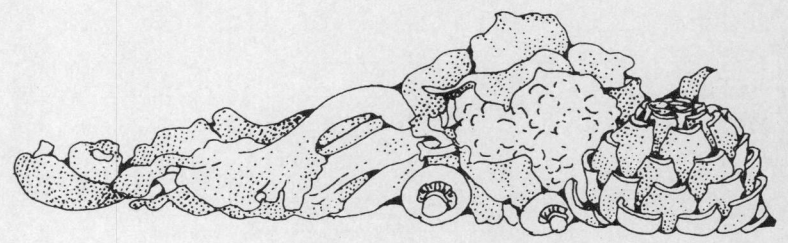

Salads

Salads — Continued

"Just For Notes"

Stuffed Mushrooms

16 large fresh mushrooms
¼ C. chopped green onions
¼ C. oleo
1 oz. crumbled blue cheese

⅓ C. dried stuffing mix
Salt and pepper to taste
1 T. white wine or enough to
suit taste

Remove stems and chop finely. Saute stems and onions in oleo. Add blue cheese and melt. Add stuffing mix, salt, pepper and wine. Fill mushrooms and bake at 350° for 15 minutes.

Beans Salad

1 can green beans or 2 C. frozen
or fresh (cooked)
1 can yellow, wax beans or 2 C.
frozen or fresh (cooked)
1 small can green limas or 1 C.
fresh or frozen (cooked)
1 C. cooked kidney beans

1 C. cooked garbanzo beans
(chick peas)
⅓ C. diced celery (opt.)
¼ C. diced onions
¼ C diced green peppers (opt.)
1 T. chopped pimento (opt.)

1½ C sugar (or less to taste)
½ C. salad oil

1 C. vinegar
Salt, pepper to taste (opt.)

Mix drained beans with other vegetables in a large bowl. Heat remaining ingredients to boiling. Pour hot over bean mixture. Refrigerate. Make the day before serving. Keeps up to 10 days.

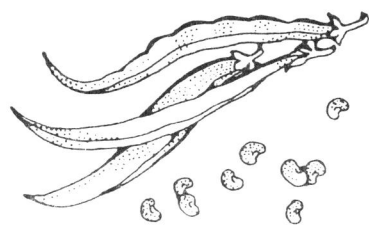

Spring Salad

1 pkg. lemon gelatin
1 C. hot water
1 small onion
1 medium cucumber

1 scant C. Miracle Whip
1 lb. carton cottage cheese
Pinch of salt

Dissolve gelatin in hot water and partially chill. Chop onion and unpeeled cucumber very fine. Mix all ingredients and add to gelatin. Chill until set.

Jello Vegetable Salad

2 (3 oz. ea.) pkgs. lemon Jello
2 C. hot water
1¼ C. mayonnaise or 1 C.
    mayonnaise & ¼ C. Cool Whip
1 C. cottage cheese

¾ C. finely chopped celery
1 C. finely chopped or shredded
    carrots
2 T. chopped onion
1 chopped green pepper

Dissolve Jello in the hot water and let set until slightly thickened. Add remaining ingredients and refrigerate.

Cucumber Jello

1 box lemon or lime Jello
1¼ C. boiling water
1 C. shredded cucumbers

1 onion (shredded)
1 T. vinegar
½ tsp. salt

Dissolve Jello in boiling water and cool. Add cucumbers, onion, vinegar and salt. Refrigerate.

7-Up Salad

1 C. applesauce
½ C. orange juice

1 pkg. lime Jello
1 small bottle 7-Up

Heat applesauce and orange juice. Dissolve Jello in it and cool. Add 7-Up and refrigerate.

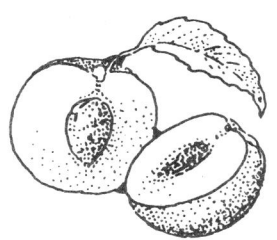

Apricot Delight

SALAD:
2 (3 oz. ea.) pkgs. orange gelatin
3 bananas (sliced)

32 miniature marshmallows
1 large can apricots (drained)

TOPPING:
1 C. liquid drained from apricots
1 egg
2 T. cornstarch

½ C. sugar
1 C. heavy cream (whipped)

For Salad: Dissolve gelatin according to package directions. Mix in remaining ingredients. Chill until firm.

For Topping: Combine all ingredients except whipped cream. Cook until thickened. Cool. Fold in whipped cream. Spread over gelatin mixture.

Strawberry Salad

3 small boxes strawberry Jello
3 C. boiling water
2 (10 oz.) boxes frozen strawberries

1 (12½ oz.) can crushed pineapple
3 large bananas (sliced)
1 C. dairy sour cream

Dissolve Jello in boiling water. Add strawberries. Stir until thawed. Add crushed pineapple and bananas. Pour ½ of mixture into 9 x 13-inch pan and chill until firm. Spread evely with sour cream. Pour remaining gelatin mixture on top and chill till firm.

Applesauce Salad

1 box strawberry Jello
1 C. hot water

2 T. red cinnamon candies
2 C. applesauce

Dissolve Jello in hot water, add candies and stir constantly until dissolved. Add applesauce. Set in refrigerator to cool. May be cut in squares and placed on lettuce leaf.

Ambrosia

1 (20 oz.) can chunk pineapple
1 (11 oz.) can mandarin orange
  segments
1½ C. seedless grapes
1 C. miniature marshmallows

1 C. flaked coconut
½ C. nuts
½ C. dairy sour cream
1 T. sugar (opt.)

Drain pineapple and oranges. Wash grapes and drain well. Mix pineapple, oranges, grapes, marshmallows, coconut and nuts. Mix sour cream and sugar together, stir into fruit mixture. Chill. Makes 4-6 servings. If desired, substitute fresh orange pieces for mandarin orange segments and then use half shells of oranges for serving dishes.

Orange Layer Salad

1 pkg. orange gelatin
1 C. boiling water
1 small can mandarin oranges
  (drained)

1 sliced banana
Juice from oranges plus cold water
  to make ¾ C.
1 C. whipped cream or Dream
  Whip

Dissolve Jello in hot water. Add juice and cold water. Chill until slightly thick. Fold in whipped cream, oranges and banana slices. Put in Jello mold and chill till firm. Before serving, remove Jello from mold. Salad will have set in layers. Can be garnished with whipped cream, coconut and fruit.

Chicken Salad

3 C. cubed chicken
1 C. diced celery
1 tsp. salt

3 hard-boiled eggs
3 sweet pickles
Mayonnaise (as desired)

Mix all together and add mayonnaise as desired for moistness. Serve on lettuce leaf and garnish with olives.

Marinated Tomatoes

4-6 tomatoes (quartered)
1 onion (sliced)
1 green pepper (sliced)
1 cucumber (sliced

1 C. oil
1 C. vinegar
1 C. sugar
Salt & pepper

Mix oil, vinegar, sugar, salt and pepper. Pour over vegetables and let marinate in refrigerator at least ½ day.

Quick Salad

1 can chunk pineapple (drained)
2 small cans mandarin oranges
(drained)

1 can peach pie filling
1 C. sliced bananas or any other
fruit desired

Mix entire contents together. Can be kept over day or 2 as acid in peach pie filling prevents bananas from turning dark.

Seafoam Salad

1 pkg. raspberry Jello
1 pkg. frozen raspberries (drained)
2 (3 oz. ea.) pkgs. cream cheese

2 T. milk
1 C. whipped cream or Cool Whip

Drain frozen raspberries and save juice. Add enough water to reserved juice to make 1 cup. Boil and add Jello. Beat cream cheese with milk until smooth. Gradually beat in hot gelatin. Chill until slightly thickened. Fold in raspberries and whipped cream. Chill until firm.

Orange Salad Supreme

1 (3 oz.) pkg. orange Jello
1 (3 oz.) pkg. orange tapioca
pudding
1 (3 oz.) pkg. instant vanilla pudding

2 C. boiling water
1 large container Cool Whip
1 (11 oz.) can mandarin oranges

Dissolve orange Jello, tapioca pudding and vanilla pudding into the boiling water. Cook until thick and bubbly. Cool. Fold in Cool Whip and add oranges; chill.

Cabbage Salad

3 C. sugar
2 C. vinegar
1 C. water
2 medium heads of cabbage
2 T. salt

1 bunch of celery
2 green peppers (1 can be red)
Carrots
1 tsp. celery seed
1 tsp. mustard seed

Boil sugar, vinegar and water for 3 minutes; let cool. Shred cabbage. Add salt and let stand for 1 hour. Squeeze out excess water. Grind celery, peppers, carrots, celery seed and mustard seed. Mix with drained cabbage and pour cooled liquid over cabbage. Will keep for 3 weeks in refrigerator in sealed jars. Makes 3 quarts.

Angel Hash Salad

1 (16 oz.) can crushed pineapple
1 (16 oz.) can fruit cocktail
2 T. cornstarch
¼ C. sugar
2 bananas (sliced)

1 C. syrup from fruit
2 beaten egg yolks
1 medium container Cool Whip
¼ C. chopped walnuts or pecans
2 C. miniature marshmallows

Drain the pineapple and fruit cocktail; reserve syrup, set aside. Combine in saucepan the cornstarch and sugar. Add egg yolks and 1 C. reserved syrup from fruit. Blend well. Cook until thick over heat, stirring constantly. Cool thoroughly. Fold in Cool Whip, nuts, marshmallows, pineapple and fruit cocktail. Chill overnight. Before serving, add the bananas.

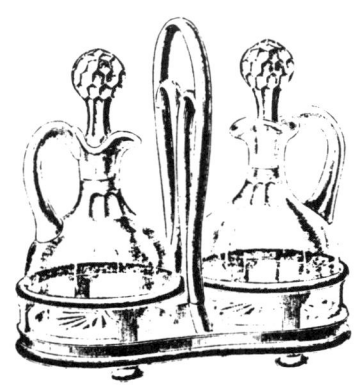

Sauerkraut Salad

1 (16 oz.) can sauerkraut	1 C. sugar
1 C. chopped celery	¼ tsp. salt
½ C. chopped onion	Dash of pepper
1 chopped green pepper	¼ C. white vinegar
1 small jar chopped pimentos	

Drain sauerkraut and chop fine. Mix remaining ingredients and chill thoroughly. Serve with a slotted spoon to eliminate juice. Place each serving on lettuce. Refrigerate in airtight container.

Frozen Cranberry Salad

1 lb. cranberries (ground)	10-12 snipped marshmallows
2 C. sugar	½ C. nuts
1 small can crushed pineapple	1 pt. whipped cream

Combine cranberries and sugar; let stand for 2 hours. Add a small can of crushed pineapple (drained) and the marshmallows, nuts and whipped cream. Stir well and freeze. Thaw in refrigerator for a few hours before serving. Can be refrozen.

Vegetable Salad

1 can whole kernel corn
1 can French-style green beans
1 can peas
1 C. chopped celery
1 C. chopped onion

1 C. chopped green pepper
¾ C. vinegar
1 C. sugar
1 tsp. salt
1 T. water

Drain corn, beans and peas. Mix with remaining vegetables. Boil vinegar, sugar, salt and water. Let cool and pour over vegetables. Let stand overnight. Will keep at least 2 weeks in refrigerator.

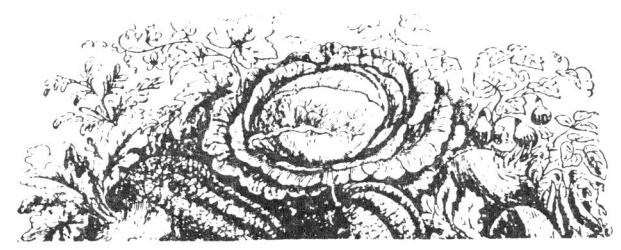

Cauliflower And Broccoli Salad

1 head of cauliflower
1 bunch of broccoli
1 red onion

⅓ C. sugar
⅓ C mayonnaise
⅓ C. oil

Wash and cut into pieces the cauliflower, broccoli and onion. Mix sugar, mayonnaise and oil. Pour over vegetables and marinate overnight.

Cabbage Salad

1 head of cabbage
1 onion
1 red onion
1 green pepper

1 C vinegar
1 C. sugar
Celery seed

Shred cabbage, onion and peppers. Salt down and let set at least 2 hours, then drain. Boil vinegar, sugar and celery seed. Cool and pour over cabbage. This will keep a long time in refrigerator.

Macaroni Salad

1 pt. mayonnaise
1 C. vinegar
1½ C. sugar
1 can Eagle Brand milk

1 lb. twist macaroni
1 green pepper (chopped)
2 grated carrots
1 chopped onion

Cook macaroni according to directions on package; drain. Stir mayonnaise, vinegar, sugar and milk until smooth. Fold in macaroni and vegetables. Cover tightly and refrigerate for 3 to 4 hours or overnight.

Three Bean Salad

1 can green beans
1 can yellow wax beans
1 can red kidney beans
1 green pepper (chopped)
1 medium onion (chopped)
¾ C. celery (chopped)

¾ C. sugar
½ C. oil
½ C. vinegar
1 tsp. salt
1 tsp. pepper

Drain beans and add remaining vegetables. Combine sugar, oil, vinegar, salt and pepper; pour over the beans. Let stand overnight.

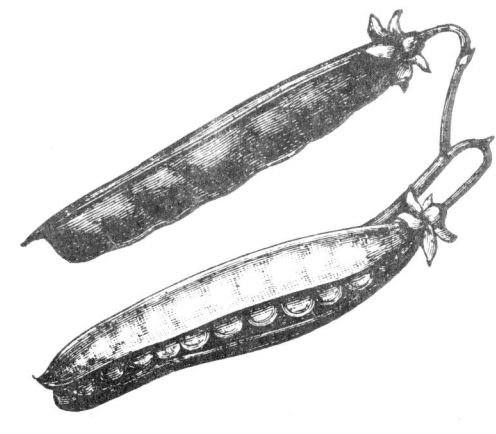

24 Hour Cabbage Salad

1 head cabbage (shredded)   1 tsp. salt
1 green pepper (chopped fine)   1 tsp. mustard seed
½ C. vinegar   1 tsp. celery seed
2 C. sugar

Mix all together and let stand 24 hours in refrigerator. Will keep 8-10 days.

Vegetable Combo

1 head of cauliflower (chopped)   1 C. sour cream
1 bunch of broccoli (chopped)   1 C. mayonnaise
2 carrots (sliced)   1 pkg. garlic salad dressing mix or
15 radishes (sliced)   Hidden Valley Dressing (mixed
2 cucumbers (sliced)   according to pkg.)

Combine cauliflower, broccoli, carrots, radishes and cucumbers. Mix sour cream, mayonnaise and garlic salad dressing. Add this dressing just before serving.

Garden Salad

2 C. diced cauliflower   1 C. vinegar
2 C. diced celery   ¼ C. salad oil
2 C. shredded carrots   ½ C. sugar
1 C. sliced radishes   1 tsp. salt
1 C. drained peas   ¼ tsp. pepper

Mix all vegetables together. Mix vinegar, oil, sugar, salt and pepper. Fold into vegetables and refrigerate. Can be made 2 days ahead of time for use.

Potato Salad

6 large potatoes (boiled & cooked)   Salt and pepper
4 hard-boiled eggs (cooled)   Salad dressing
1 small onion

Dice or better yet, slice potatoes and then take a sharp knife and slice through several times until cut as desired. Cube eggs and onion; add to potatoes. Salt and pepper, to suit taste. You can add a dash of celery seed too. Now for the dressing, use a blend of ½ Miracle Whip, ½ homemade dressing or if in a hurry take the Miracle Whip and stir in some sugar and cream (milk or Half & Half may be used) until you have the right consistency and taste (you will have to sample it).

Broccoli & Cauliflower Salad

1 head of cauliflower   1 C. mayonnaise
1 pkg. radishes   ¼ C. milk
2 C. frozen peas   1 pkg. Hidden Valley original
2 T. dried onion flakes   dressing

Break cauliflower and add peas, radishes and onion flakes; set aside. Mix mayonnaise, milk and dressing. Combine with vegetables. Pour into pan and refrigerate.

Pineapple Salad

1 lg. can pineapple chunks (drained)   1½ C. water
Pineapple juice drained from fruit   1 C. sugar
    3 T. cornstarch

Mix pineapple juice, water, sugar and cornstarch. Bring to a boil and boil until clear. Add pineapple chunks. Mix with 3 oranges and 4 bananas (cut up). Chill before serving.

Cranberry Salad

2 C. ground cranberries
2 C. sugar
2 pkg. lemon-flavored gelatin
4 C. warm water

1 C. diced celery
1 C. broken nut meats
1 orange (ground)

Combine cranberries and sugar and let stand. Dissolve lemon gelatin and water; chill until partially set, add all other ingredients and let stand until firm. (Serves 10-12).

Cherry Salad

1 can cherry pie filling
1 can fruit cocktail
¼ C. nuts

1 C. miniature marshmallows
½ C coconut (opt.)

Drain the fruit cocktail but leave cherry pie filling as it is and mix together and chill. Two cups chopped apples may also be added, if desired.

Cherry Pie Filling Salad

1 can cherry pie filling
1 can mandarin oranges
1 can chunk pineapple

Small pkg. marshmallows
1 small container Cool Whip

Drain liquid from mandarin oranges and pineapple. Mix all ingredients together and chill.

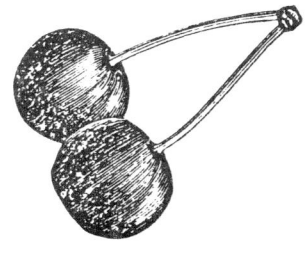

Cheese Salad

1 small can crushed pineapple	1 C. hot water
½ C. sugar	¾ C. grated cheese
1 lemon or 4 T. lemon juice	½ pt. whipping cream
1 pkg. lemon Jello	½ can pementos (opt.)

Boil for 3 minutes pineapple, sugar and lemon juice. Dissolve Jello in hot water and combine two mixtures. When Jello stars to congeal, stir in cheese and whipped whipping cream and pimentos. Refrigerate until serving time.

Cream Cheese Lime Mold

1 (No. 2½) can pears	¾ C. whipping cream or 1 pkg.
3 oz. pkg. Philadelphia cream	Dream Whip
cheese	½ C. pecans
1 box lime Jello	

Drain pears. Dice the pears and heat the juice. Dissolve Jello in the hot juice. Add cheese, softened to room temperature and blend well. Cool. Add the cut up pears and pecans, then fold in whipped cream or Dream Whip. Pour into mold and chill until serving time.

Deli Salad

1 bunch broccoli (chopped)	1 onion (chopped)
1 (5 oz.) can water chestnuts	½ lb. fresh mushrooms (sliced)
(sliced)	1 C. Italian salad dressing
1 can olives (green or black,	(regular or low-calorie)
chopped)	

Marinate vegetables in salad dressing several hours or overnight. Drain before serving. You can add some chopped tomato just before serving if you wish.

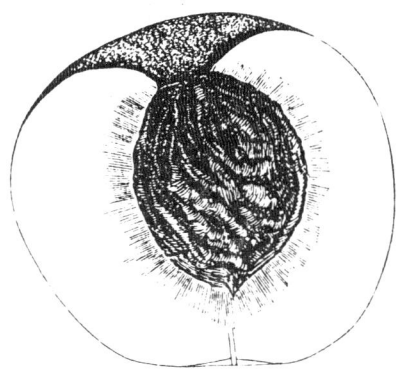

Fruit Salad

1 (29 oz.) can sliced peaches
1 (15½ oz.) can pineapple chunks
1 (11 oz.) can mandarin orange
   segments
3 C. liquid (juice from fruits plus
   enough water to make 3 C.

1 (3 1/8 oz.) pkg. (not instant)
   vanilla pudding mix
1 (3½ oz.) pkg. (not instant)
   tapioca pudding mix

Drain fruit (keep juice). Stir and combine pudding mixes and 3 C. liquid. Microwave on full power until it boils (about 6-8 minutes) and turns clear and thick. Cool and add drained fruit. Keeps well in refrigerator. (OPTIONAL: Add bananas, fresh strawberries, etc.)

Lime Salad

2 pkgs. lime Jello (fix according to directions; let harden)

BLEND TOGETHER:
1 (8 oz.) pkg. cream cheese
1 (12 oz.) pkg. Dream Whip
1 can crushed pineapple (drained)

Marshmallows
Maraschino cherries
Nuts (opt.)

Overnight Lettuce Salad

1 head lettuce (cut up)
½ C. celery (chopped)
½ C. green pepper (chopped)
1 onion (sliced)
1 pkg. frozen peas (do not thaw)

1 C. mayonnaise
2 T. sugar
4 oz. grated cheddar cheese
8 slices bacon (fried crisp and crumbled)

Layer the first 5 ingredients in an oblong pan. Spread with mayonnaise. Sprinkle with sugar. Then add the cheese and bacon. Refrigerate, covered with foil, overnight.

Pistachio Salad

1 sm. box pistachio instant pudding
1 (20 oz.) can crushed pineapple and juice

2 C. miniature marshmallows (white or colored)
1 sm. carton Cool Whip
¼ C. pecans (opt.)

Mix all ingredients together and refrigerate.

SOUPS

Soups

Mulligan Stew

1 lb. stew meat
1 tsp. salt and pepper
1 can tomato soup

Carrots (sliced)
Potatoes (diced)
Onions (diced)

Put stew meat in pan and saute over medium heat. Add the salt and pepper. Add the can of soup and 2 cans water. Cook until meat is done. (I use my 4 qt. pressure cooker. Bring it to top ring and pressure 20 minutes.) Add as many carrots, potatoes and onion as you need for your size family. Cook without pressure cooker until vegetables are done. If your stew seems runny, cook awhile with lid off pot.

Chicken Stew

1 broiler-fryer chicken
2 chicken bouillon cubes
4 potatoes (scrubbed and peeled)
3 medium onions (chopped)
4 carrots (sliced crosswise)

1 bag or bunch spinach
1½ C. skim milk
2 tsp. salt
½ tsp. pepper
¼ tsp. Tabasco sauce (opt.)

Cook chicken in water until tender, save broth, remove chicken from bon (discard skin, fat and bone). Cook vegetables in broth with 2 bouillon cubes added (except spinach) until tender. Mash potatoes, add chicken meat to broth and vegetables. Add spinach, milk, salt and Tabasco sauce. Heat through, but do not overcook spinach. Serves 6-8.

Cheese Soup

1 C. water
1 large potato (shredded)
1 medium onion (chopped)
1 medium carrot (grated)
1 stalk celery (finely chopped)

1 C. chicken consomme' or broth
(or use 2 tsp. chicken bouillon
dissovled in 1 C. hot water)
½ C. Half and Half
1½ C. shredded sharp cheddar
cheese (about 6 oz.)

Combine water, potato, onion, carrot and celery in 2 qt. casserole; cover. Microwave at high (100%) until potatoes are tender, 12-17 minutes, stirring after half the cooking time. Stir in consomme' and Half and Half; cover. Microwave at medium-high (70%) until heated through, 6-8 minutes. Mix in cheese, stirring until melted.

Easy Clam Chowder

2 cans potato soup
2 cans clam chowder soup
1 can minced clams

1 can evaporated milk
2¾ C. milk
¼ C. butter

Mix together and cook until hot.

Hamburger Soup

1 lb. hamburger
2 tsp. salt
¼ tsp. pepper
1 C. diced carrots
½ C. diced onion

1 C. diced potatoes
¼ C. rice
5 C. water
2 C. tomato juice

Brown hamburger and drain. Mix hamburger with remaining ingredients. Simmer 1 hour.

Vegetable Beef Barley Soup

3 T. salad oil
2 lbs. beef chuck (cut into ¾-inch
   cubes; I use stew meat)
2 C. chopped onions
1 tsp. minced garlic
½ tsp. thyme
½ tsp. marjoram
6 C. water

2 cans (about 14 oz. ea.) beef
   broth
1½ C. diced carrots
¾ C. diced celery
1½ tsp. salt
½ tsp. freshly ground pepper
3 C. diced potatoes
¾ C. barley

In large pot, heat oil over medium high heat. Add meat and cook, stirring occasionally, until browned on all sides. Add onions, garlic, thyme and marjoram. Cook, stirring, 10 minutes more. Add water, beef broth, carrots, celery, barley*, salt and pepper. Bring to a boil; reduce heat and simmer uncovered 1½ hours. Add potatoes. Bring to a boil; reduce heat and simmer uncovered 30-40 minutes, until potatoes are tender. (*If using quick barley, add with the potatoes.) Makes 14 C., 225 calories per cup.

Beef Stew

⅔ C. flour
1½ tsp. salt
½ tsp. pepper
3 lbs. boneless stew beef (cut in
   1-inch cubes)
4 T. fat or oil
6 C. water

6 medium-size onions (sliced)
8 medium-size potatoes (cut in
   1-inch cubes)
10 medium-size carrots (quartered)
3 C. frozen peas (if desired)
4 stalks celery (cut up)
¼ C. water

Combine flour, salt and pepper. Coat meat with seasoned flour. Save remaining flour. Brown meat in hot fat in a 4-qt. saucepan. Add water and cover tightly. Simmer until meat is tender, about 1½ hours. Add onions, potatoes, celery and carrots. Cover and simmer until all vegetables are tender. Blend ¼ C. water with remaining flour. Add to stew, stirring gently. Cook until thick. Serves 12.

Beef Stew

2 lbs. beef stew meat or a roast
(cut into 1-inch cubes)
4 medium onions (sliced)
¼ C. soy sauce
¾ tsp. salt
½ tsp. pepper

4-6 large diced potatoes
4 large carrots (cut into chunks)
1 celery (opt.)
3 T. flour
Water

Put sliced onions and meat in bottom of small roaster. Pour enough water over this to cover well. Add soy sauce. Mix flour, salt and pepper together. Pour over water and mix well. May be lumpy but these will cook out. Bake covered for 1 hour at 350°. Add carrots and celery. Bake for another ½ hour, then add potatoes. Bake for another hour or until done. Add more water if necessary. If more water is added, add some additional flour to keep broth thick. Makes 6-8 servings.

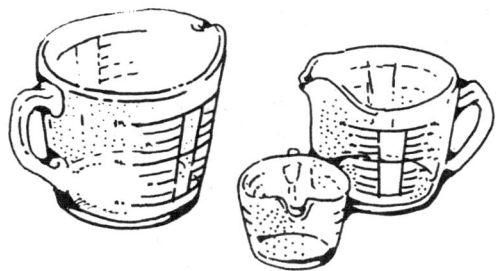

Broccoli-Cauliflower Soup

1 lb. fresh broccoli (cut in
small pieces)
1 lb. fresh cauliflower
(cut in small pieces)
2 chicken bouillon cubes

½ C. margarine
1 medium onion (chopped)
½ C. flour
4 C. milk
2 C. shredded cheddar cheese

Boil broccoli, cauliflower and chicken bouillon cubes in a 3-qt. saucepan with just enough water to cover, until vegetables are just tender, approximately 3 minutes. Meanwhile, saute ½ C. margarine and 1 medium chopped onion in a ½-qt. saucepan. Add ½ C. flour and mix. Add 4 C. milk and cook over medium heat until thickened. Add mixture to vegetables, after they have been boiled. Add 2 C. shredded cheddar cheese. Heat until cheese melts through. Season with salt and pepper and serve. Yield: Serves 4-6.

Vegetable Chowder

2 C. diced potatoes
¾ C. diced onions
½ C. diced celery
½ C. diced carrots
2½ C. boiling water
2 tsp. salt
4 T. flour
4 T. oleo (melted)

2 C. milk
½ tsp. pepper
½ tsp. dried mustard
½ T. minced parsley
¼ lb. grated cheddar cheese
1 C. canned tomatoes with pinch
    soda in them
¼ C. sugar (to suit taste)
1 can creamed corn

Put potatoes, onions, celery and carrots in boiling water with salt. Cook until tender. In saucepan mix flour and oleo together. Add milk and mix well. Add pepper, mustard, parsley and cheese. Pour cooked vegetables and sauce together. Add tomatoes, sugar and creamed corn. Heat well and serve. Freezes well.

'Just For Notes"

MAIN DISHES

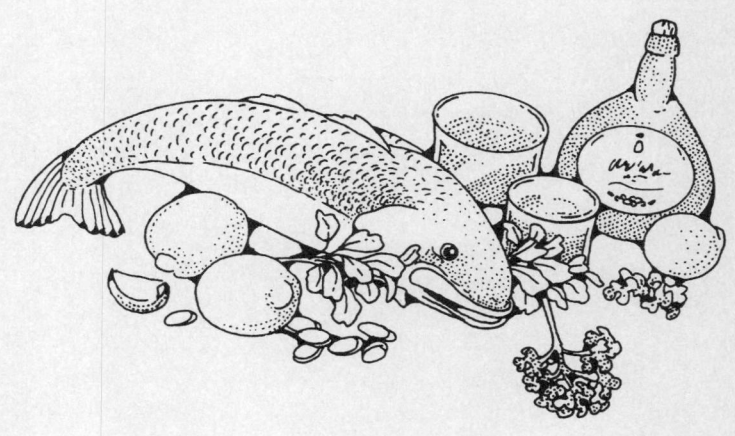

Main Dishes

Main Dishes - Continituted

"Just For Notes"

Easy 5-Hour Roast

Large roast (round bone steak)   1 pkg. dry onion soup
1 can mushroom soup

Place roast on heavy foil. Cover with undiluted mushroom soup and sprinkle dry onion soup over this. Cover entire roast with foil and secure edges tightly. Place on cookie sheet (to prevent drippings from spilling in oven). Then place in oven at 275° for 5 hours or more. No peeking while cooking.

Plum Chicken

4 chicken breasts (boned & skinned)   1 T. dry sherry
1 C. plum jelly   ¼ tsp. garlic powder
3 T. soy sauce   ¼ tsp. ginger
    1 (20 oz.) can pineapple chunks

Cut chicken into chunks. Marinate overnight in plum jelly, soy sauce, sherry, garlic powder and ginger. Drain pineapple. Place pineapple chunk with a chunk of chicken on round toothpick. Bake 10-12 minutes in 400° oven. Serve at once.

Salmon Ball

1 lb. can salmon (drained)   1 tsp. horseradish
1 (8 oz.) pkg. cream cheese   ¼ tsp. salt
   (softened)   1/8 tsp. liquid smoke
1 T. lemon juice   2 tsp. grated onion

Mix all together.

Beef Sandwiches

2 lbs. cooked beef (thinly sliced)
1 (10½ oz.) can beef consomme
½ C. ketchup
¼ C. water
1 onion (thinly sliced)

1 green pepper (cut in strips)
1 large garlic clove (mined)
1 tsp. Italian seasoning
1 loaf French bread (halved
   lengthwise)

Combine consomme, ketchup, water, onion, green pepper, garlic and Italian seasoning in large saucepan or electric skillet. Bring to a boil and add beef, cover tightly and cook slowly for 15 minutes. Drain off and reserve cooking liquid; dip cut surfaces of bottom and top halves of bread in the liquid. Place hot beef and vegetables on bottom halves and cover with tops of bread. Serve remaining liquid with sandwiches.

Sausage And Potatoes

1½ lbs. red potatoes (diced)
1½ lbs. sausage (diced, bratwurst's
   good)
¼ C. chopped green pepper
½ C. chopped green onion

Salt and pepper to taste (opt. not
   needed with the sausage)
½ C. chopped celery
1 tsp. dill weed
1 tsp. parsley

Saute potatoes and sausage in a skillet about 5 minutes. If not enough grease, add a small amount of oleo. Add the other ingredients and simmer for 15 minutes. Add 15 minutes to cooking time if using coarse ground sausage.

Barbecue Beef Sandwiches

3-4 lbs. beef roast (cooked & sliced) *1 T. horseradish*
2½ C. ketchup *1 T. Worcestershire sauce*
½ C. brown sugar *1 tsp. garlic salt*
½ C. vinegar

Mix all ingredients, except beef and bring to a boil, then simmer for about 15 minutes. Pour over beef and place in oven or microwave until beef is thoroughly warmed. Serve on buns.

Beef And Noodle Hot Dish

1½ lbs. ground chunk *1 medium onion (chopped)*
1 can cream of chicken soup *1 (8 oz.) pkg. noodles*
1 can cream of mushroom soup *¼ lb. Velveeta cheese (grated)*
1½ C. milk *1 bottle stuffed olives (sliced)*

Cook noodles and drain. Brown meat and the onion, season with salt and pepper to taste. Combine the noodles and meat mixture, adding the milk and soup. Pour into a buttered casserole. Top with cheese and the olives. Bake for 45 minutes to 1 hour at 350°. May sprinkle with chow mein noodles and return to oven for 5 minutes.

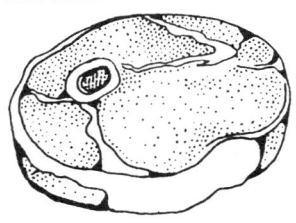

Goulash

1½-2 C. uncooked macaroni *1 small jar spaghetti sauce*
1 lb. ground beef *1 can mushrooms*
1 can Veg-All *Mozzarella cheese (shredded)*

Cook macaroni and drain. Brown and drain ground beef. Mix all ingredients and top with cheese.

Beef Stroganoff

½ C. minced onion
1 clove garlic (mashed)
¼ C. butter
1½ lbs. ground beef
2 T. flour

Salt and pepper to taste
1 (4 oz.) can mushrooms
1 can cream chicken soup
1½ C. sour cream

Saute onion, garlic and butter. Add meat and brown. Add flour, salt, pepper and mushrooms. Cook 5 minutes. Add soup, simmer uncovered for 15 minutes. Stir in sour cream and heat through gently. Serve over cooked noodles or rice.

Potato-Fish Casserole

3 large potatoes (halved crosswise)
1 lb. fresh or frozen fillets of fish
1 T. lemon juice
½ tsp. salt (divided)
1 medium-large onion (sliced)
1 medium green pepper
  (seeded, sliced)

1 medium pepper (re, opt.)
1-2 tomatoes (sliced)
2 tsp. margarine
½ tsp. white or regular pepper
Pimiento slices for garnish
1 can cream of potato soup

Cook potatoes, covered, in 1-inch boiling water for 20-25 minutes until tender but not crumbly; drain. Peel and cut into 1/8-inch slices. Arrange fillets in single layer in shallow dish; sprinkle with lemon juice and ¼ tsp. salt. Let stand 30 minutes. In shallow 2-qt. casserole, arrange layer of sliced potatoes. Layer half the onions and pepper slices over potatoes. Place fish fillets over the vegetables in a single layer. Sprinkle with ¼ tsp. salt and pepper. Repeat layer of peppers, onions, sliced tomatoes and top casserole with remaining potatoes. Dot with margarine. Garnish with pimiento*. Bake at 350° for 30 minutes or until fish is flaky. Makes 4 servings. (*Pour undiluted cream of potato soup over all ingredients. Cover for first 20 minutes, uncovered 10 minutes.)

Pizza

1 Chef-Boy-Ar-Dee cheese pizza
1½ lbs. hamburger
1 C. uncooked macaroni
1 small can mushroom pieces

1 medium size can pizza sauce
1 pkg. sliced pepperoni
1 can cream of mushroom soup
3 C. mozzarella cheese

Make pizza crust according to instructions on box. Bake until almost done. Brown hamburger, cook macaroni. Drain hamburger and macaroni. Place on pizza crust in the following order; hamburger, macaroni, cream of mushroom soup, can of pizza sauce from the pizza mix, mushrooms, sliced pepperoni, other can of pizza sauce, top with mozzarella cheese. Bake in 400° oven for 15-20 minutes.

Helen's Meat Balls

3-4 lbs. ground beef
½ tsp. salt
1 tsp. Lawry's Seasoning Salt
½ C. chopped onion

½ C. catsup
2 eggs for every pound of meat
½ C. oatmeal for every pound
of meat

SAUCE:
2 C. catsup
2 C. brown sugar

¼-½ C. red wine vinegar
2-3 tsp. dry mustard

Mix as you would a meat loaf. Roll into balls. Place in 300° oven with foil over pan. Bake about 1½-2 hours, depending on size of balls. About 15 minutes before serving time, drain off excess grease. Pour sauce over the top of meat balls. Continue baking without foil for the remainder of the baking time.

Beef Burgundy

3 lbs. round steak or boneless beef
   chunk (cut into 1½-inch long
   slices)
2 cans golden mushroom soup
3 beef bouillon cubes
1 C. burgundy wine

2 medium onions (sliced thin)
2 green peppers (sliced)
1 tsp. garlic powder
1 T. salt-pepper
1½ pkgs. egg noodles

Mix all ingredients in large casserole dish (except noodles). Cover and bake 2-3 hours. Serve over hot buttered egg noodles.

Favorite Egg-Sausage Casserole

1½ lbs. ground sausage
9 eggs
½ tsp. dry mustard

1½ C. grated cheddar cheese
3 slices bread (cubed)
3 C. whole milk

Brown sausage; drain. Beat eggs slightly. Combine rest of ingredients. Place in ungreased 9 × 13-inch pan. Refrigerate. Take out 1 hour before baking. Bake at 350° for 45 minutes. (If not put out ahead of time, bake at 300° for 1½ hours.)

Creamed Tomatoes

MIX TOGETHER IN PAN:
¼ lb. oleo
¼ C. sugar

¼ C. flour

Add to mixture above 1 quart of tomatoes, heat until boiling. Add 1 C. cooked macaroni.

Turkey Dressing Sandwiches

1 medium turkey (7-10 lbs.)	1 lb. hamburger (browned)
4 loaves bread (21 slices each) or	1 lb. unseasoned pork sausage
24-26 C. bread cubes	(browned)
1 small can sage	1 large onion (diced)

Boil turkey until done. Cool and remove turkey from bone. Reserve broth for later use. In large roaster combine bread (torn into pieces) and turkey broth until desired moistness is reached. Add turkey, sage, hamburger, sausage and onion. Mix all well. Roast in oven at 350° until hot all the way through. Serve on buns. Can be used as a main dish also. Works well in crock pot also.

Easy Chicken Dinner

2 pkgs. frozen broccoli	1 C. mayonnaise
2 C. cooked chicken or 3 chicken	1 tsp. lemon juice
breasts (steamed, boned and	½ C. shredded cheese
sliced)	½ C. soft bread crumbs
2 cans cream of chicken soup	Onion rings

Steam chicken breasts; cool and bone and slice. You may use fresh broccoli. Clean and line pan. Combine soup, mayonnaise, cheese. Place chicken slices on broccoli; pour soup mixture over all, then bread crumbs and onion rings on top. (Soup, mayonnaise and cheese may be heated to shorten cooking time.) Bake about 30 minutes at 350°.

Chicken And Dressing Casserole

1 double box Stove Top stuffing	1 can cream of chicken soup
1 large pkg. California blend vegetables (frozen)	12 oz. sour cream
	2 C. cubed cooked chicken
1 can cream of mushroom soup	1 C. grated cheddar cheese

Mix the dressing according to package directions. Place into large cake pan. Put frozen vegetables over the top. Combine the soups with the sour cream. Add the chicken and stir well. Pour over the dressing and vegetables. Bake at 350° for 30 minutes.

Grandmother's Swiss Steak

2 lbs. round or sirloin (cut 2'' thick)	1 medium onion (sliced)
½ C. flour	½ green pepper (chopped fine)
Dash of salt	1 C. boiling water
¼ C. ham or bacon grease	1 can canned tomatoes

Mix flour and salt; pound into meat. Heat bacon or ham grease. Fry meat and brown on both sides; drain grease. Add peppers, onion and tomatoes. Pour on meat and bake at 350° for 2 hours.

Chunk Chicken Casserole

1 (7 oz.) pkg. macaroni	½ tsp. celery salt
1 (10¾ oz.) can cream of chicken	1 tsp. Worcestershire sauce
soup	1 (6¾ oz.) can chunk chicken
1 C. shredded cheddar cheese	(flaked apart)

Prepare macaroni according t package directions. Drain. Heat together soup, milk, cheddar cheese, celery salt, Worcestershire sauce. Add flaked chicken. Add mixture to cooked macaroni. Pour into a greased 2-qt. baking dish. Bake in a preheated oven at 350° for about 45 minutes (until hot and bubbly).

Chicken Biscuit Dinner

¼ C. margarine	1⅓ C. chicken broth
⅓ C. flour	¾ C. milk
½ tsp. salt	2 C. cubed cooked chicken
Dash pepper	1 C. cooked peas
⅓ C. chopped onion (opt.)	1 C. cooked carrot slices
1 can refrigerator biscuits	Poppy seed (if desired)

In 10-inch ovenproof skillet, melt margarine; blend in flour, salt and pepper. Add chicken broth and milk. Cook, stirring until thickened. Add chicken, onion, peas and carrots. Simmer until bubbly. Separate biscuits. Arrange over chicken mixture. Sprinkle with poppy seed if desired. Bake at 375° for 20-25 minutes or until biscuits are golden brown. Serves 5-6.

99 LBS. NET WEIGHT

WHOLE BEAN
UNCOATED

TABLE RICE

Chicken And Rice Casserole

3 C. cooked, diced chicken
2 cans cream of chicken soup
1 C. mayonnaise
2 C. very finely diced celery
3 C. fluffy cooked rice

1 tsp. dried onion flakes
2 T. lemon juice
1 tsp. salt
4 hard-boiled eggs (diced)

Mix; put into greased 9 x 13-inch pan. Sprinkle with ½ C. slivered almonds and 2 C. crushed, buttered corn flakes (¼ C. oleo). Bake at 350° for 1 hour, until lightly browned.

Chicken Casserole

3 C. cooked chicken (diced)
½ C. chopped celery
1 can crema of mushroom soup
1 (3 oz.) can chow mein noodles

¼ C. chopped onions
1 C. evaporated milk
1 can chicken rice soup
⅓ C margarine (melted)
½ C. Pepperidge Farm dressing

Combine ingredients and bake 1 hour at 350°.

Spread-A-Burger

1½ lbs. ground beef
1 can tomato soup
⅓ C. finely chopped onion
1 T. prepared mustard
1 T. Worcestershire sauce
Green peppers or mushrooms (opt.)

1 tsp. prepared horseradish
1 tsp. salt
Dash of pepper
Mozzarella cheese
1 loaf French bread
1 C. grated cheddar cheese

Fry the ground beef and drain off excess grease. Mix all the ingredients together, leaving the mozzarella to put on top. Cut the French bread in half the long way. Spread the mixture on each half and cover edges completely. Place aluminum foil around the buns but leave the top open. Sprinkle grated mozzarella cheese over the top. Bake at 350° for 15-20 minutes.

Pepper Steak For Four

2 lbs. round steak (sliced thick and cut into 2-inch squares)
6 large green peppers (sliced lengthwise)
1 large onion (sliced)
16 oz. pkg. fresh mushrooms (sliced)

1 small glass of cooking wine (juice glass)
1 small can tomato sauce
1 small can water
1 large clove garlic (cut up in small pieces)

Brown meat in small amount of oil with garlic. Add salt, pepper and Italian seasonings to taste. Add tomato sauce, wine and water. Cover and let simmer ½ hour. Add peppers, onions and mushrooms. Cover and let simmer 1½ hours or until tender. (I serve this with regular and wild rice mix.)

Green Pepper Steak

1 lb. beef chunk or round
(fat trimmed)
¼ C. soy sauce
1 clove garlic
2 stalks celery (thinly sliced)
1 T. cornstarch
¼ C. salad oil

1 C. green onion (thinly sliced)
1 C. red or green pepper (cut into
1-inch strips)
1½ tsp. grated fresh ginger
1 C. water
2 tomatoes (cut into wedges)

With a very sharp knife cut beef across grain into thin strips 1/8-inch thick. Combine soy sauce, garlic, ginger. Add beef, toss and set aside while preparing vegetables. Heat oil in large frying pan or wok. Add bef and toss over high heat until browned. Taste meat. If it is not tender, cover and simmer for 30-40 minutes over low heat. Turn heat up and toss until vegetables are tender-crisp, about 10 minutes. Mix cornstarch with water. Add. Stir and cook until thickened. Add tomatoes and heat through.

Meat Balls Supreme

1½ lbs. hamburger
½ C. milk
2 tsp. salt
1 C. catsup
½ C. water
¼ tsp. Worcestershire sauce

3 T. onion (chopped)
2 T. vinegar
⅓ C. brown sugar
Dash of Tabasco sauce
½ tsp. pepper

Shape hamburger, milk, salt and pepper into meatballs and brown. Combine remaining ingredients and bring to boil. Place meat balls in casserole dish and cover with sauce. Bake in 325° oven 1-1½ hours until sauce is thick.

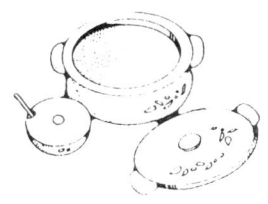

Ground Beef And Wild Rice

4 C. boiling water
1 C. raw wild rice
1 (4-6 oz.) can sliced mushrooms
    (drained)
1 can cream of mushroom soup
1 can cream of chicken soup
2 cubes beef bouillon dissolved in
    1 C. water

1 bay leaf (crumbled)
¾ C. chopped celery
⅓ C. chopped onion
1½ lbs. lean ground beef
¼ tsp. each celery salt, garlic salt,
    onion salt, paprika, pepper
½ C. slivered almonds

Pour water over rice and let stand 15 minutes. Add remaining ingredients except almonds. Saute celery and onion in small amount of butter and add to above mixture. Brown ground beef. Drain and add to rice and sauce. Pour into casserole. Sprinkle with almonds. Bake 1½ hours in moderate oven (350°). Serves 8-10 persons.

Round Steak With Creme

2 lbs. beef round steak (cut ¼-inch
    thick)
¾ C. chablis or other dry white
    wine
1 T. water
¾ C. flour
½ tsp. paprika

4-6 T. butter or margarine
    (or more)
1 egg
1 beef boullion cube
1 tsp. salt
2 T. chopped parsley
2 C. Half and Half

On cutting board, pound steak to 1/8-inch thickness with a meat mallet. Cut steak into small pieces (2×2-inches). Beat egg and water until blended. On waxed paper, combine flour, salt and paprika. Dip steak in egg, then in flour mixture. In a large skillet, over low heat, melt butter or margarine. Increase heat to medium and brown pieces a few at a time until brown on both sides (3-4 minutes). Adding more butter if needed. Remove meat to warm platter and keep warm. In same skillet, over medium heat, stir in Half and Half, wine and bouillon cubes, scraping to loosen brown bits from bottom. Cook over low heat 3-4 minutes to thicken slightly, stirring constantly. Serve sauce over steak. Sprinkle with parsley. Makes 8 servings.

Dang Good Beef

2 lbs. flank steak
2 green peppers
2 T. olive or salad oil
1 tsp. salt
¼ C. soy sauce
1 (1 lb.) can bean sprouts

2 tomatoes
1 clove garlic
Dash pepper
¼ tsp. ground ginger
½ tsp. sugar
1 T. cornstarch
¼ C. water

Cut flank steak in thin strips across grain. Cut tomatoes in quarters. Trim away seeds and ribs from peppers and cut in big chunks. Heat oil in large skillet. Add strips of beef, crushed garlic, salt, pepper and ginger. Fry over high heat until brown on all sides. Season with soy sauce and sugar. Cover tightly and cook slowly for 5 minutes. At this point toss in tomatoes, peppers and drained and rinsed bean sprouts. Bring to boil and cook briskly 5 minutes. Make paste of cornstarch and water. Add to beef mixture and cook until thickened slightly. Stir occasionally. Makes 6 servings.

Swiss Steak With A Difference

1½-2 lbs. round steak
¼ C. flour
1 tsp. salt
Shortening

1/8 tsp. pepper
1 (10¾ oz.) can mushroom soup
1 (10½ oz.) can onion soup

Combine flour, salt and pepper. Pound into steak with a meat hammer or edge of heavy saucer. Cut into serving portions. Brown steak on both sides in hot shortening. Arrange meat in lightly greased 9 × 1342-inch pan. Combine soups; pour over meat. Cover and bake in 325° oven about 1½ hours or until tender. Serve the soup mixture as gravy over potatoes, rice or noodles. Yield: 6-8 servings.

Pepper Steak

1 lb. chopped steak	1½ medium green pepper
4 T. cooking oil	1 large onion
¼ C. soy sauce	2 T. flour
Chopped tomatoes may be added	1 C. cold water
during cooking for variety in taste	Cooked rice

Brown chopped steak in oil on medium heat. Add soy sauce, cover and simmer for 15 minutes. Add green pepper cut into slices and onion cut in sliced lengthwise. Cover and simmer 15 minutes. Add flour stirred in cold water until lumps are gone. Pour over ingredients in pan, stirring as you pour. Simmer 20-30 minutes. Serve over cooked rice. Serves 4-6 people.

Beef Ribs

1 C. cider vinegar	½ C. honey
2 T. Worcestershire sauce	½ C. catsup
1 tsp. salt	1 tsp. dry mustard
1⅓ tsp. black pepper	1 clove garlic (minced)
4 lbs. beef ribs	

Combine all ingredients except the ribs in a saucepan. Bring ribs to a boil, then reduce heat. Cover and simmer 15 minutes. Arrange the rimbs in a single layer in baking pan. Pour hot marinade over meat. Cover and let stand 1 hour. Drain, reserving the excess marinade. Bake the ribs at 350° for 1 hour or until tender. While cooking turn ribs frequently and baste with marinade. Serves 4.

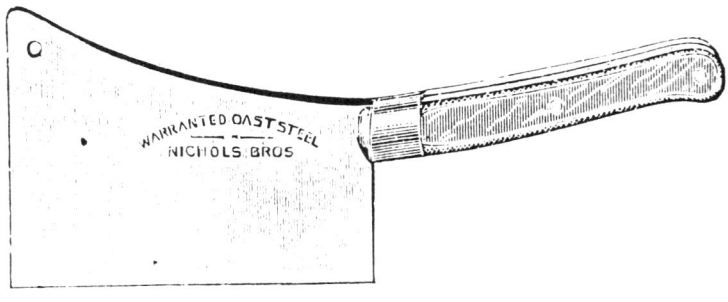

Minute Steak

4 minute steaks
2 tsp. butter
1 (8 oz.) can tomato sauce

1 clove garlic (minced)
½ tsp. dried basil
Mozzarella cheese

Brown minute steak on both sides in butter. Add garlic and basil in tomato sauce and pour over minute steaks. Cover and simmer over very low heat for at least ½ hour. Top each steak with mozzarella cheese. Cover and allow cheese to melt. Makes 4 servings.

Pork Chops 'N Stuffing

4 pork chops
3 C. soft bread crumbs
2 T. chopped onions
¼ C. melted butter

¼ C. water
¼ tsp. poultry seasoning
1 can mushroom soup
⅓ C. water

Brown chops and place in baking dish. Lightly mix together bread crumbs, butter, ¼ C. water, onion and poultry seasoning. Place a mound of stuffing on each chop. Blend soup with ⅓ C. water and pour over chops. Bake at 350° for 1 hour.

Green Pepper Steak

1 lb. beef chuck roast or round
steak (trim fat)
¼ C. soy sauce
1 clove garlic
1½ tsp. grated ginger
¼ C. salad oil (peanut oil)

1 C. green onions (sliced)
1 C. green peppers (cut in
squares)
1 T. cornstarch
1 C. water
2 tomatoes (cut in wedges)

Cut beef across grain into thin strips 1/8-inch thick. Combine soy sauce, garlic, ginger and add beef. Toss and set aside. Heat oil in wok or large skillet. Add beef and toss over high heat until browned. (If meat is not tender, cover and simmer for 30-40 minutes over low heat.) Add vegetables and toss over high heat until tender crisp. Mix cornstarch with water and add to meat and vegetables. Stir and cook until thickened. Add tomatoes and heat through. Serve over rice or noodles. Serves 4. We have enjoyed adding cauliflower, carrots, broccoli and sugar pea pods to this basic recipe.

Marinated Chicken/Rice Dish

2 chicken breasts (deboned)
¼-½ C. olive oil
1 tsp. garlic
1 tsp. thyme
¼ tsp. pepper

¾ C. wild rice
¼ C. short grain brown rice
2-2½ C. chicken stock
6-10 fresh mushrooms
¼ C. green peas

Do ahead: If you buy 2 whole breasts (unboned), the reserve after fileting should get you about enough stock for this recipe. Mix oil, garlic, thyme and pepper in airtight container. Thoroughly submerse chicken in liquid. Cover and refrigerate at least 24 hours. May be cooked a variety of ways. Pan frying is good but a little dry. (I like microwave a lot, about 10-12 minutes. I'll put a slice of cabbage over the chicken just to help hold the heat in.) Bring stock in pan to boil, add rices. Cook 20-25 minutes. Mix mushrooms and peas in 5 minutes before done.

Barbecued Venison Chops Or Steaks

1 lb. venison
1 medium onion (chopped)
½ C. celery (chopped)
2 T. butter or margarine
1 C. ketchup
1 C. water

2 T. brown sugar
2 T. vinegar
3 T. Worcestershire sauce
¼ C. lemon juice
Salt
Pepper

Dredge venison in flour and brown. Place in baking dish. Saute onion and celery in butter until tender. Add remaining ingredients, stir and cook on medium until flavors are well blended, about 15 minutes. Pour over venison and bake at 350° for 1½ hours.

Steamed Fish

1 fish (any kind, at least 1 lb.) Salt
¼ C. softened butter Pepper
1 T. lemon juice Bay leaf

Clean fish, rub with salt and pepper. Prepare lemon butter by mixing lemon juice and butter. Grease sheet of brown paper well on both sides. Place fish on paper and spread with lemon butter. Roll fish in paper and secure well. Dip newspapers in water and roll around fish until about 12 thicknesses. Place in a cavity in the middle of a bed or coals. A 1 lb. fish will cook in about 20 minutes. Allow 10 additional minutes for each extra pound. Cook about ½ lb. fish per person.

Baked Fish

1 lb. fish fillets 1 small can mushrooms
2 T. lemon juice ½ C. chopped onion
¼ C. butter 2 T. parsley
½ C. cracker crumbs 4-5 slices bacon

Lay the fish in casserole and sprinkle with the lemon juice. Melt the butter; add cracker crumbs. Mix and pour on fish. Add the mushrooms, onion and parsley. Cover with bacon. Bake in 400° oven for 30-35 minutes. Bake uncovered and baste every 10 minutes.

Beer Batter

1 egg 2 tsp. sugar
⅔ C. beer 2 tsp. salt
¼ C. oil ¾ C. flour

Blend ingredients together and dip fish in batter; fry in hot oil.

Tartar Sauce

1 pt. mayonnaise
½ bunch parsley
¾ lb. onion
½ pt. dill pickles
¼ head cabbage

½ green pepper
1/16 bottle horseradish
¼ bunch celery
¼ oz. celery salt

Chop all of the above ingredients and blend thoroughly in blender. Makes 1 quart.

Golden Fry Batter

½ C. corn oil
1 C. flour

1 egg
1½ C. milk

Blend oil and flour. Add egg and milk. Beat with rotary beater until smooth. Batter will be thin. Take 2½ pounds cut-up chicken or equal amount of fish (wash and drained), and then coat with unseasoned flour. Dip pieces into batter, letting excess drip off. Fry in oil (375°), 3 to 4-inches deep until golden brown and tender. Drain on absorbent paper. Season and serve.

Pan Fried Fish

Fish (fresh or frozen)
Salt and pepper

Milk
Potato flakes (instant)

Dip whole or cut fish in milk and then in potato flakes. Fry in hot oil until done or pan fry. Salt, to taste.

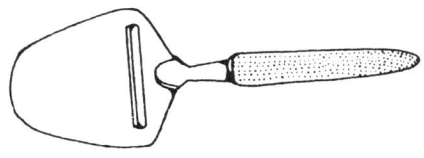

Baked Fish

1 C. flour
2 tsp. paprika
1/8 tsp. garlic salt
1 tsp. soda
Dash of salt and pepper

2 eggs
2 T. milk
1 lb. fish fillets
½ C. margarine

Mix dry ingredients together in plastic bag. Then beat eggs with milk. Dry off fillets and dip in egg mixture. Shake well in flour mixture. Melt margarine. Place fish in lightly greased jelly roll pan and pour melted margarine over it. Bake at 350° for 20 minutes on each side. Turn fillets over once.

Salmon Loaf

1 large can salmon
4 T. butter
1 C. cracker crumbs
1 egg

½ C. milk
1 tsp. salt
2 small onions

Mix and pour into buttered pan. Bake 1 hour in medium oven.

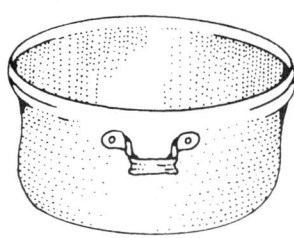

Swedish Potato Bologna

10 lbs. beef
8 lbs. pork
8 lbs. potatoes (par-boiled)

2 lbs. onions
2-3 T. poultry seasoning
1 T. (heaping) salt and pepper

Put all the above ingredients through sausage grinder twice, alternating ingredients so that they are thoroughly mixed. Put in casings and freeze until ready to use. Boil and serve.

Country Fried Chicken

1 fryer (cut up)
1 T. salt

3 C. water

1 tsp. Italian seasoning
2 tsp. onion salt
2 tsp. seasoned salt

2 envelopes instant chicken broth
¼ tsp. seasoned pepper
1 C. flour

Cover chicken with water and salt; chill for 1 hour. Combine seasoning and flour. Drain chicken and shake in flour mixture until thickly coated. Fry in 1-inch of shortening in a fry pan at 375° for 5 minutes on each side. Remove and blot off excess grease with paper towel. Place in covered casserole or roaster and bake at 300° until done.

Oven Crisp Chicken

¼ C. butter or oleo
1 C. potato flakes
2 T. dry onion flakes
½ tsp. chili powder

¼ C. Parmesan cheese
1 egg
2 T. milk

Melt the oleo and pour into cake pan or cookie sheet. Salt the chicken pieces and dip the chicken in mixture of 1 egg and the 2 T. milk. Mix all the dry ingredients together. Roll the chicken in potato mixture. Place skin side down in the buttered pan. Bake at 350° for 1½ hours. Turn chicken halfway through cooking time.

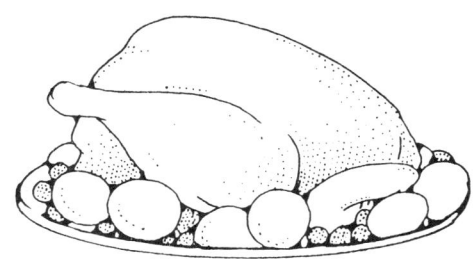

Crispy Baked Fillets

1 lb. fish fillets (your choice)
Season salt
Lemon and pepper seasoning

2 T. oil
⅓ C. corn flake crumbs

Preheat oven to 500°. Wash and dry fillets and cut into serving pieces. Season and dip in oil and coat with corn flake crumbs. Arrange in a single layer in a lightly oiled shallow baking dish. Bake 10 minutes without turning.

Stuffed Chops

6 Iowa chops
1 box Stove Top dressing (pork)

Cut an opening about ½ down opposite the bone side of chops. Prepare Stove Top dressing as directed. Then stuff chops and place in a covered baking dish for 1½ hours at 325°. Wonderful!

Broccoli-Rice Hot Dish

2 pkgs. frozen broccoli
1 C. raw rice
½ C. chopped onions
½ C. chopped celery

1 T. butter
1 (8 oz.) jar Cheese Whiz
1 can cream of mushroom soup
1 can cream of chicken soup

Cook broccoli according to directions on package. Cook rice according to directions on package. Cook (simmer) onion, celery and butter until tender. Mix together Cheese Whiz, mushroom and chicken soups. Put in casserole, rice, broccoli, onion, celery, butter mixture. Then stir in cheese-soup mixture. Bake at 350° for 30 minutes, stirring twice.

Ham Rolls

1½ lbs. ground ham
¾ lb. ground pork
¾ lb. ground beef
1½ C. crushed cracker crumbs

2 eggs (beaten)
1 C. milk
Dash of pepper

SAUCE:
½ C. vinegar
½ C. water

1½ C. brown sugar
1 T. dry mustard

Mix the first ingredients very well. Mix into egg shaped balls and place in baking dish. Make sauce and pour over balls. Cover casserole and bake at 350° for first hour, turn to 325° and bake 1 hour more, basting several times with sauce.

HORSERADISH TOPPING:
1 beaten egg
3 T. sugar
1 T. (heaping) flour

½ C. cider vinegar
½ C. water
1 T. butter

Mix all ingredients and cook about 5 minutes, stirring constantly. Cool. When ready to serve whip 1 pkg. Dream Whip and add 1 T. horseradish. Add to above mixture and serve over ham balls.

Maidrites Oink

1½ lbs. ground pork (browned)
½ C. ketchup
¼ C. BBQ sauce

½ tsp. Worcestershire sauce
2 T. brown sugar
¾ of a tube of Ritz crackers
(crushed)

Combine all ingredients and simmer in fry pan for 15-30 minutes. The Ritz crackers make them stick together and not crumble.

Sharon's Meatloaf

2 lbs. groung chuck
1 egg
1 tsp. salt
¼ tsp. pepper
½ tsp. leaf basil
½ tsp. thyme
¼ tsp. catsup

2 tsp. prepared mustard
1½ C. bread crumbs
2 beef bouillon cubes in 1 C.
   boiling water
½ C. finely chopped celery
½ C. chopped onion
1 C. shredded cheddar or Swiss
   cheese

Mix all ingredients and bake at 375° for 60-70 minutes.

Delicious Meatloaf

1½ lbs. ground beef
¾ C. quick oatmeal
¼ C. onion (chopped)
1½ tsp. salt
¼ tsp. pepper

1 C. tomato juice
1 egg
Brown sugar
Catsup

Mix all ingredients except brown sugar and catsup. Place in bread pan. Spread mixture of brown sugar and catsup on top. Bake at 350° for 1 hour and 15 minutes.

Blue Cheese Meatloaf

1½ lbs. hamburger (chuck)
1 C. dried bread
1 C. milk
1 egg
1 small onion (chopped)
1 T. Worcestershire sauce

½ tsp. dry mustard
¼ tsp. pepper
¼ tsp. ground sage
1 clove garlic
2 oz. crumbled blue cheese
1½ tsp. salt

Soak bread in milk. Mix all ingredients. Spread in ungreased loaf pan, 9×5×3-inches. Cook uncovered in 350° oven about 1½ hours.

Meatloaf

1½ lbs. ground beef
1 C. tomato juice
¾ C. oatmeal
1 egg (beaten)

¼ C. onion (chopped)
1½ tsp. salt
¼ tsp. black pepper

Put in loaf pan. Sprinkle a little brown sugar on the top. Bake for 1 hour at 350°.

Cabbage Dish

1 head cabbage
2 C. medium white sauce

1 large cream cheese
Buttered bread crumbs

Chop and cook cabbage until tender. Drain and put in baking dish. Prepare white sauce and melt cream cheese in it. Pour sauce with melted cream cheese over cabbage. Top with buttered bread crumbs. Bake at 350° until it looks hot and bubbly.

Swedish Meatballs

3 lbs. hamburger
2 eggs
Salt and pepper

1½ C. oatmeal
Onion (if desired)

Mix all together and if too stiff, can add another egg or a little milk. Make into bite-size balls and brown in hot fat. Take balls out of drippings and make gravy. put balls back into gravy. Simmer until ready to serve being very careful so that they don't scorch.

Swiss Steak With Mushrooms

½ C. flour
Salt and pepper
2 lbs. round steak (1-inch thick)
3 T. bacon drippings or other fat
1 medium onion

1 clove garlic (minced, opt.)
1 C. celery (chopped)
1 C. tomato juice or ½ C. catsup
and ½ C. water
1 sm. can mushrooms (undrained)

Mix flour with a little salt and pepper. Pound mixture into steak on both sides. Heat fat in large heavy skillet or Dutch oven, brown steak. Add remaining ingredients, season to taste with salt and pepper. Cover and bake in moderate oven, 350°, about 1½ hours or until steak is tender. Turn and baste steak occasionally and add a little water if needed to keep gravy from becoming too thick.

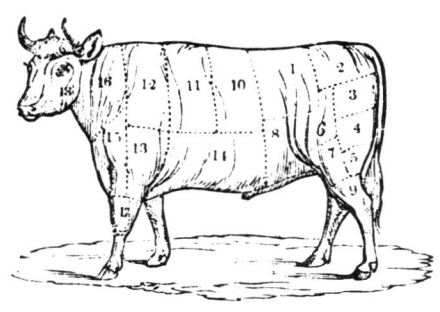

Vegetables Casserole

1 (32 oz.) pkg. frozen French fries
1 (16 oz.) pkg. frozen mixed
  vegetables
1 can celery soup

1 (8 oz.) jar Cheese Whiz
½ C. chopped onions
½ C. chopped green peppers

Pour mixed vegetables in glass-flat, 2-qt. size casserole. Saute in margarine the chopped onions and green pepper. Pour over the frozen veggies; spread can of celery soup on top. Spread jar of Cheese Whiz on top also. Then lay frozen French fries over all, heaping high. Bake in oven 45 minutes or until fries are nice and brown.

Corn Bread Casserole

1 can cream corn
1 can drained whole kernel corn
2 eggs (slightly beaten)
1 small carton sour cream (½ pt.)

1 stick margarine (melted)
4 T. diced onion
1 box Jiffy corn bread mix
Salt and pepper to taste

Mix all ingredients together and bake in greased pan (uncovered) at 350° for 45 minutes or until golden brown.

Party Potatoes

10 large potatoes
8 oz. sour cream
8 oz. cream cheese

Salt and pepper
Garlic salt (opt.)

Boil potatoes until done. Mash thoroughly. Add sour cream and cream cheese, salt and pepper to taste. Garlic is optional. Beat all together thoroughly. Put into greased casserole. This can be frozen and reheated and still tastes fresh.

Potato Casserole

1 (32 oz.) pkg. frozen hash browns
1 can cream of chicken soup
1 small carton sour cream
½ C. chopped onion

1½ C. cubed Velveeta cheese
½ C. melted butter
Salt and pepper

Mix ingredients in casserole dish. Bake 45-60 minutes in 350° oven. Top with cracker crumbs or corn flake crumbs 15 minutes before done baking. (Stir mixture a couple of times while baking.)

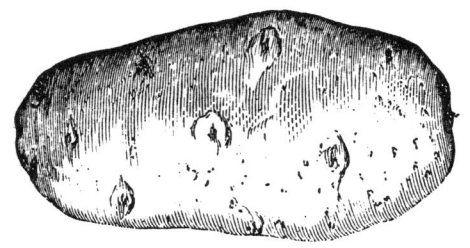

Potatoes Are Cheaper

½ stick margarine
1 pint sour cream
1 can cream of chicken soup
1 tsp. salt

2 C shredded cheddar cheese
½ C. diced onion
2 lbs. bag hash browns

Mix all ingredients. Bake in buttered 9 × 13-inch pan at 350° for 30-40 minutes.

Au Gratin Cheese Potatoes

Cook 8-9 medium potatoes with peeling. When cold, peel and grate. Heat 1 C. Half and Half, ½ C. butter or margarine, 1 tsp. salt. Pour over potatoes in greased 9 × 13-inch loaf pan. Top with 8 oz. mild cheddar cheese. Bake 40-45 minutes in 350° oven.

Fried Green Tomatoes

BATTER:

1 C. cornmeal	1 T. sugar
½ C. flour	Pinch of pepper
2 tsp. baking powder	1 C. milk
1 tsp. salt (or less)	

6-8 green tomatoes

To Fry: Cut tomatoes into ¼-inch slices. Dip in batter and fry in deep fat, drain and serve.

Spaghetti Pie

6 oz. spaghetti	2 well beaten eggs
⅓ C. grated Parmesan cheese	1 lb. ground beef or bulk pork
1 C. cottage cheese (8 oz.)	sausage
½ C. chopped onion	¼ C. chopped green pepper
1 (8 oz.) can (1 C.) tomatoes	1 (16 oz.) can tomato paste
(cut up)	1 tsp. dried oregano (crushed)
1 tsp. sugar	½ C. shredded mozzarella cheese
½ tsp. garlic salt	(2 oz.)
2 T. butter or margarine	

Cook the spaghetti according to package directions; drain. (Should have about 3 C. spaghetti.) Stir butter or margarine into hot spaghetti. Stir in Parmesan cheese and eggs. Form spaghetti mixture into a ''crust'' in a buttered 10-inch pie plate. Spread cottage cheese over bottom of spaghetti crust. In skillet cook ground beef or pork sausage, onion and green pepper until vegetables are tender and meat is browned. Drain off excess fat. Stir in undrained tomatoes, tomato paste, sugar, oregano and garlic salt; heat through. Turn meat mixture into spaghetti crust. Bake, uncovered, in 350° oven for 20 minutes. Sprinkle the mozzarella cheese atop. Bake 5 minutes longer or until cheese melts. Makes 6 servings.

Baked Corn

2 eggs
1 T. flour
1 T. sugar
8 soda crackers (put on top)

1 can cream style corn
1 T. melted butter
½ tsp. salt
½ C. milk

Beat eggs, add corn and rest of ingredients in order given. Crush soda crackers and put on top. Bake in greased casserole for 30 minutes at 375° and 30 minutes more at 350° until golden brown.

Corn Casserole

2 C. uncooked macaroni
1 lb. ground beef
1 can cream style corn
Salt

1 T. vegetable oil
1 medium onion (chopped)
1 can cream of mushroom soup
Pepper

Cook macaroni in 2-qts. water with the oil. Brown ground beef and onion. After draining macaroni, mix all ingredients together. If necessary it can be thinned with a small amount of milk. Bake at 325° for 30 minutes.

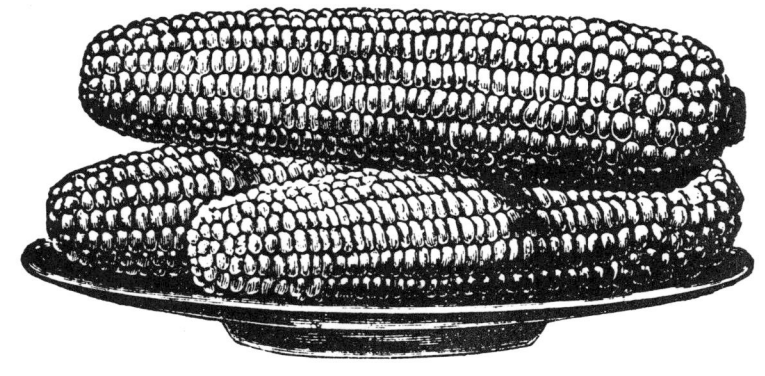

Country Company Potatoes

8 medium potatoes
1 can cream of chicken soup
½ C. butter
1½ C. cheddar cheese (grated)

1 (8 oz.) box sour cream
⅓ C. onion (minced)
1 C. corn flakes crumbs
2 T. butter

Boil potatoes with jackets on and cool. Peel and grate. Place in baking pan, 9 × 13-inch. Blend can of soup and butter. Heat until butter melts. Add cheese, sour cream and onion. Pour mixture over potatoes and top with corn flakes and 2 T. butter. Bake at 350° for 45-60 minutes uncovered.

Creamy Potato Hot Dish

12 medium potatoes (peeled, cooked
    mashed with milk)
8 oz. sour cream
¼ C. butter or margarine

8 oz. cream cheese (softened)
½ tsp. onion salt
Paprika

Mix softened cream cheese and sour cream with mashed potatoes. Melt butter, add onion salt. Pour over potato mixture. Sprinkle with paprika. Bake at 325° for 30 minutes.

"Just For Notes"

BREADS

Breads

Bubble Bread

2 loaves of frozen bread
1 C. brown sugar
1 tsp. cinnamon
1 pkg. reg. butterscotch pudding
(not instant)

½ C. milk
2 tsp. vanilla
1 stick margarine (melted)

Thaw and cut the bread dough into 1 to 2-inch cubes. Layer in ungreased 9 x 13-inch cake pan. Mix the brown sugar, cinnamon, pudding mix, milk, vanilla and melted margarine. Pour over bread crumbs and let rise. Bake at 350° for 30 minutes or more until done. Turn upside down on serving tray.

Apricot Coffee Bread

¾ C. oleo
1 C. sugar
1 tsp. vanilla
3 eggs
3 C. flour

4 tsp. baking powder
½ tsp. salt
2 tsp. grated lemon rind
½ C. milk
¼ C. apricot preserves

Cream together the oleo, sugar and vanilla. Add eggs, beating well after each one. Sidt together the dry ingredients. Combine the milk and apricot preserves. Add milk mixture alternately with dry ingredients to the creamed mixture and blend after each addition. Grease and flour a 10-inch Bundt pan. Spread ⅓ of batter on the bottom of the pan. Sprinkle ⅓ C. coconut and ¼ C. chopped nuts on batter, not allowing them to come to edge of pan. Top with ½ remaining batter. Sprinkle with ⅓ C. coconut and ¼ C. chopped nuts. Cover with remaining batter. Bake at 350° for 40-45 minutes. Cool in pan for 10-15 minutes and remove from pan. Heat ¼ C. apricot preserves and 1 T. water in small pan. Remove from heat and stir in 1½ C. powdered sugar. Drizzle over top of slightly warm bread, allowing glaze to drip down sides. Sprinkle coconut over frosted top.

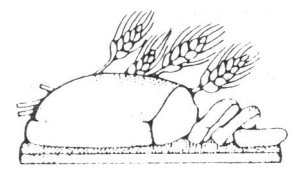

Whole Wheat Bread

2 pkgs. yeast	6 T. shortening
3 C. warm water	4 C. unsifted stoneground whole
4 C. white flour	wheat flour
4 T. white sugar	2 C. pumpernickle rye flour
2 T. salt	2 C. additional white flour
1 C. packed brown sugar	

Dissolve the yeast in the 3 C. of warm water. Add flour, sugar and salt. Let rise in a warm place until and bubbly, about 20 minutes. Combine the brown sugar, shortening and 1 C. of hot water. Let cool to lukewarm and add to risen mixture. Add whole wheat flour, the pumpernickle rye flour and the remaining 2 C. of white flour. Mix as long as you can, then turn mixture onto table and knead for at least 15 minutes. Place in buttered bowl. Cover and let rise in warm place for 1 hour or until double in bulk. Turn onto a well floured table again and separate mixture into 4 balls. Let rise in pans, in warm place, covered with a towel, for about an hour or until light. Bake at 350° for 1 hour. Remove from pans and place on racks to cool. Butter to of bread while hot and store in plastic bags in refrigerator.

Swedish Rye Bread

2 cakes compressed yeast	4 T. molasses
4 T. melted shortening	1 T. salt
1 tsp. sugar	3 C. rye flour and rest white flour
1 C. brown sugar	Fennel seed or caraway if desired
1 qt. lukewarm water	

Dissolve yeast in lukewarm water to which 1 tsp. sugar has been added. Add enough white flour to make soft dough. Let stand in a warm place until bubbly. Heat molasses and add a pinch of soda, then add melted shortening to sponge with molasses-soda mixture. (Be sure it isn't too hot kill the yeast.) Add sugar, salt and rye flour, Beat well. Add white flour to make stiff dough. Grease bowl and let rise double. Knead down and let rise again. Make 4 loaves and leat rise agian and bake. (I put the fennel seed in when I add molasses shortening to sponge. This is a must at holiday time in our home and during winter months.)

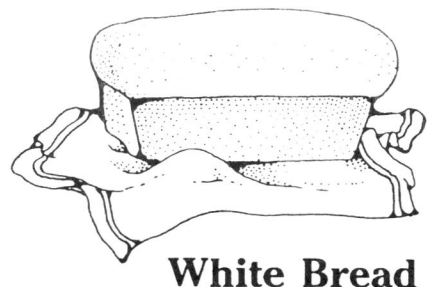

White Bread

2 C. milk
5 T. sugar
1½ T. salt
5 T. lard

2 C. lukewarm water
2 pkgs. yeast
12-13 C. flour

Scald milk and add lard, sugar and salt. Cool till lukewarm. Dissovle yeast in lukewarm water and add to lukewarm milk mixture. Beat in 6 C. flour until smooth. Gradually add remainder (6-7 C.) until dough forms a ball and is stiff enough to be kneaded. Turn out on floured board and knead quickly and lightly until smooth and elastic. Place in greased bowl, bursh with melted lard or butter, cover and let rise until double, in a warm place (will take 45 minutes to 1 hour). Divide dough into four equal portions and shape into loaves. Place in greased bread pans, cover and let rise until double in bulk, about an hour. Bake at 400° for about 50 minutes. Remove from pans and butter tops and sides.

Whole Wheat Banana Bread

2½ C. whole-wheat flour
1 C. firmly packed brown sugar
3½ tsp. baking powder
1 tsp. cinnamon
½ tsp. salt
1 C. chopped nuts

¾ C. water
½ C. instant dry milk
3 T. oil
1 slightly beaten egg
1 C. (2 med.) mashed bananas

Stir together first 5 ingredients (dry). Press sugar lumps to make small. Combine water, dry milk, oil and egg. Add to bananas and nuts, then add to dry mixture, stirring just until ingredients are blended. Turn into buttered pan. Bake at 325° for 60-70 minutes. Remove from pan and cool on rack.

Banana Bread

⅓ C. shortening
⅔ C. sugar
2 C. flour
1 tsp. soda

½ tsp. salt
2 eggs
3 mashed bananas
¼ C. sour milk

Cream shortening; add sugar, then eggs. Add rest of ingredients and mix. Bake at 350° for 1 hour.

Swedish Rye Bread

5 C. warm water
1 C. brown sugar
2 pkgs. yeast
2 tsp. salt

5 C. medium rye flour
1 C. dark molasses
6 T. lard
14 C. white flour (approx.)

Use 1 C. warm water for yeast. mix rest of water, lard, brown sugar, salt and molasses. Add rye flour and yeast. Stir in as much white flour as possible, then knead in rest to make a soft dough. Let rise twice punching down in between. Let rise until double. Shape into loaves and rise again. Bake 45-50 minutes at 350°. It takes all day to make good rye bread as you cannot hurry it.

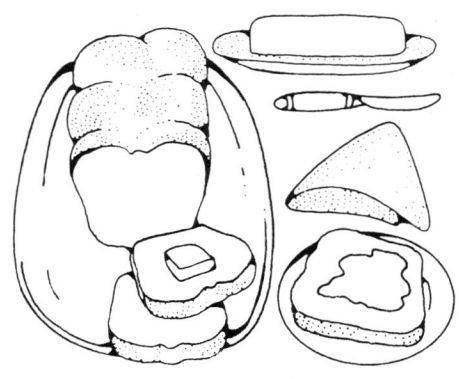

Cinnamon-Raisin Bread

2 pkgs. dry yeast
½ C. warm water
1¾ C. warm water
3 T. sugar
1 T. salt
2 T. shortening

6-7 C. Gold Medal flour
1 C. raisins
¼ C. sugar
2 tsp. cinnamon
2 T. water
Butter or margarine (softened)

Dissolve yeast in ½ C. warm water. Stir in 1¾ C. warm water, 3 T. sugar, salt, shortening and 3½ C. of the flour. Beat until smooth. Mix in raisins and enough remaining flour to make dough easy to handle. Turn dough onto lightly floured surface. Knead until smooth and elastic, about 10 minutes. Place in greased bowl. Turn greased side up. Cover and let rise in a warm place until double, about 1 hour. (Dough is ready if an indentation remains when touched.) Punch down dough and divide into halves. Roll each half into rectangle 18×9-inches. Mix ¼ C. sugar and the cinnamon. Sprinkle each half with 1 T. water and half of the sugar mixture. Roll up, beginning at 9-inch side. With side of hand, press each end to seal. Fold ends under. Place seam side down in greased loaf pan. Brush with butter. Let rise until double, about 1 hour. Bake at 350° for 25-30 minutes. Remove from pans. Brush with butter and cool on rack.

Yeast Bran Bread

½ C. sugar
¼ C. oleo
1½ tsp. salt
1 C. All Bran (Kellogg's)
1 C. boiling water

2 pkgs. yeast
1 C. warm water
2 eggs (beaten)
6-6½ C. flour

Combine sugar, oleo, salt, All Bran and boiling water. Cool. Soften yeast in warm water. Add to above mixture. Put all ingredients together and add flour; mix well. Put in greased bowl and let rise until double in bulk. Stir down and shape into 2 loaves. Let rise until double. Bake at 350° for 45 minutes.

Mom's Braided Bread

2 C. scalded milk	2 pkgs. yeast
½ C. shortening	½ C. lukewarm water
⅔ C. sugar	2 eggs (beaten)
2 tsp. salt	8 C. flour

Combine milk, shortening, sugar and salt. Cool to lukewarm. Add yeast, dissolve in water and mix well. Add eggs and stir. Add flour and mix well. Cover mixing bowl and let rise until double in bulk. Punch down and knead lightly. Divide dough into 3 parts. Next divide each part 3 times (to make 3 braided loaves). Roll each of the 9 pieces of dough into a rope shape. Spread each rope generously with butter, cinnamon and sugar before braiding ropes together. Braid 3 ropes together to make 1 log. Let rise until double in bulk. Bake at 300° for 25-30 minutes. Ice with frosting made from milk, butter, powdered sugar and almond flavoring. Garnish with pecans, red and green cherries and candied fruit. Makes 3 loaves.

Onion Bread

1 pkg. active dry yeast	2 T. sugar
1¼ C. warm water	2 tsp. salt
3 T. minced instant onion	2⅔ C. flour
2 T. shortening	

In large mixer bowl, dissolve yeast in warm water and add the minced onion. Add shortening, sugar, salt and 2 C. of the flour. Blend ½ minute on low speed, scraping bowl constantly. Beat 2 minutes medim speed, scraping bowl occaionally. Stir in remaining flour until smooth. Scrape batter from side of bowl. Cover; let raise in warm place until double, about 30 minutes. Stir down batter by beating about 25 strokes. Spread evenly in greased loaf pan. Smooth out top of bater by patting into shape with floured hand. Cover; let rise until double, about 40 minutes. Heat oven to 375°. Bake 45 minutes or until loaf sounds hollow when tapped. Brush top with melted butter. Remove loaf from pan; cool on wire rack.

CAKES 'N MUFFINS

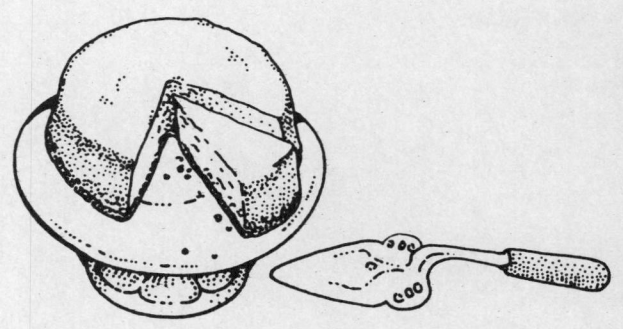

Cakes 'N Muffins

"Coffee Time" Coffee Cake

2 C. sugar
2 C. self-rising flour
3 eggs
½ tsp. salt
¼ tsp. cloves

1 tsp. cinnamon
1 C. oil
1 C. pecans
2 jars strained apricots
  (baby food)

Mix ingredients only until flour is blended. Bake in grased and floured bundt pan 55 minutes at 350°. Let stand 10 minutes. Remove from pan and sprinkle with powdered sugar while warm.

Stuffed Crescent Rolls

3 oz. cream cheese
2 T. minced onion
3 T. melted oleo

2 C. cubed chicken
1 pkg. crescent rolls
Salt and pepper to taste

Make crescent rolls into 4 pieces putting two together closing perforation. Mix cream cheese and melted oleo together until smooth. Mix remaining ingredients. Put ½ C. of mixture into center of crescent roll and close and secure seams by pinching. Brush with melted butter and crushed croutons. Bake until done, 350°, about 30 minutes or until golden brown.

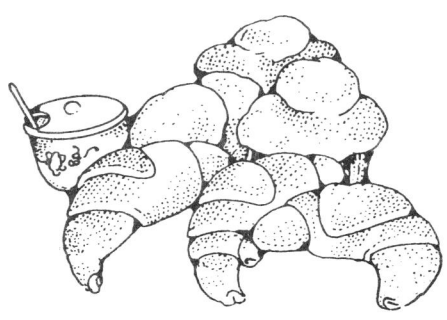

Fruit Shortcake

2 C. sifted flour
3 tsp. baking powder
1 tsp. salt
¼ C. sugar

⅓ C. Crisco or lard
1 egg (beaten)
⅔ C. milk

Mix all dry ingredients. Cut in shortening until mixture looks like coarse meal. Add milk and egg, stirring just enough to hold dough together. Place dough on board which has been dusted with flour. Knead lightly several times and roll dough about ¾-inch thick. Cut with floured cutter or just pat dough out in pie place or round cake pan. Sprinkle a little sugar on top of shortcake. Bake in hot oven, 425° for 15-20 minutes or until brown as desired.

Triple Strawberry Shortcake

1 pkg. strawberry cake mix
1 C. boiling water
16 oz. pkg. frozen sliced
   strawberries (thawed)

1 pkg. strawberry gelatin
2 C. sweetened whipped cream or
   frozen whipped topping (thawed)

Heat oven to 350°. Bake cake mix in two round 9 × 1½-inch pans, as directed on package. Cool for 10 minutes. Remove from pans. Cool cake completely. Pour boiling water on gelatin in small bowl. Stir until gelatin is dissolved. Stir in strawberries. Pour half of the gelatin mixture into each of 2 clean round pans. Refrigerate until thickened, about 30 minutes. Place cake layers over gelatin. Refrigerate until gelatin is firm, at least 4 hours. Dip 1 layer in pan into warm water for 5 seconds. Invert on serving plate, gently shaking loose. Remove remaining layers from pan as above; invert on first layer. Spread with remaining whipped topping. Serve immediately or store in refrigerator.

Dutch Cherry Cake

¼ C. melted shortening
¾ C. sugar
2 eggs (separated)
½ C. milk
1½ C. flour

3 tsp. baking powder
¼ tsp. salt
1 tsp. vanilla
2 C. cherries (drained)

SAUCE:
1 C. cherry juice
¼ C. water
1½ T. cornstarch

1 C. cherries
¼ C. sugar (or more)
1 T. butter

Mix sugar, shortening and egg yolks. Stir in dry ingredients (sifted together). alternately with the milk and vanilla. Fold in cherries and beaten egg whites. Bake at 350° for 35-40 minutes. Serve squares of cake with the sauce which is made by heating the cherry juice and sugar to boiling and then adding the 1½ T. cornstarch that has been moistened with the ¼ C. water. Cook until slightly thickened and add cherries and butter. If cherries are real sour, you may want more sugar.

Dump And Spread Cake

20 oz. can sweetened pineapple
1 can cherry pie filling
1 box white or yellow cake

1 stick margarine
½ C. chopped pecans

Dump pineapple in 9 x 13-inch cake pan. Spread evenly. Spoon cherry pie filling over and spread. Dump dry cake mix over the above and spread. Slice margarine thin over the entire cake. Sprinkle with pecans and bake at 350° for 50 minutes. Serve plain or with whipped cream.

Neopolitan Bundt Cake

1 white cake mix	*12 dros red food coloring*
1 C. water	*¼ C. chocolate syrup*
¼ C. oil	*⅔ C confectioners sugar*
3 eggs	*3 T. chocolate syrup*
1 tsp. strawberry extract	

Preheat oven to 325°. Grease and flur bundt pan. Beat white cake mix, 1 C. water, ¼ C. oil and 3 eggs. Pour ⅓ batter into pan (1⅔ C.) Put ½ remaining batter in a small bowl; stir in strawberry extract and food coloring. Carefully pour into pan. Stir chocolate syrup into remaining batter and pour into pan. Bake for 40-45 minutes.

For Chocolate Glaze: ⅔ C. confectioners sugar and 3 T. chocolate syrup. Drizzle over top.

Rhubarb Cake

1 egg	*2 C. flour*
1½ C. brown sugar (firmly packed)	*1 tsp. soda*
½ C. shortening	*¼ tsp. salt*
1 C. sour milk (add 2 T. vinegar to fresh milk in cup before you start)	*1½ C. finely diced rhubarb*

Cream sugar, egg and shortening. Add dry ingredients with milk and fold in rhubarb. Pour in 9×13-inch pan. Sprinkle with topping of:

½ C. white sugar	¼ tsp. cinnamon
½ C. nuts	

Mix together. Bake for 35 minutes in 350° oven.

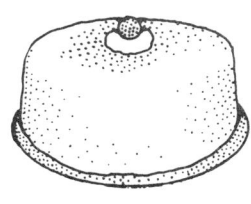

Fresh Apple Cake

CREAM: 2½ C. sugar, 1 C. oil   3 C. flour
Add 4 eggs one at a time   1 tsp. salt
7 T. orange juice   3 tsp. baking powder
2½ tsp. vanilla

In bowl combine 4 cooking apples (peeled, cored and sliced), 2 tsp. cinnamon, ¼ C. sugar. In greased and floured tube pan, layer batter, apples and ending with apples. Bake at 350° for 1½ hours. Cool in pan 5-10 minutes. Invert onto rack and immediately invert onto cake plate. Cool ½ hour before serving.

Crumb Cake

1½ C. white sugar   2 eggs
2 C. flour   ¾ C. milk
¾ C. margarine   1 tsp. vanilla
2 tsp. baking powder

Mix first 4 ingredients together and take out 1 C. Add remainder of ingredients and beat well. Pour into pan and sprinkle crumbs over top. Bake 20 minutes at 350°

Ugly Cake

1 pkg. yellow cake mix	1 (16 oz.) can fruit cocktail
2⅓ C. Bakers angel flake coconut	2 eggs
½ C. packed brown sugar	½ C. margarine
½ C. granulated sugar	½ C. evaporated milk

Mix cake mix, undrained fruit cocktail, 1 C. coconut and eggs. Mix 2 minutes. Pour into 9×13-inch greased pan. Sprinkle with brown sugar. Bake at 325° for 45 minutes. Bring last 3 ingredients to boil and boil 2 minutes. Stir in rest of coconut. Pour over cake when slightly cooled.

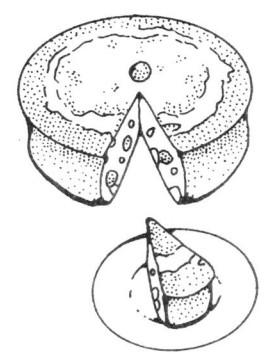

Strawberry Shortcake

2 (10 oz. ea.) pkgs. strawberries (thawed)

1 (3 oz.) pkg. strawberry Jello

BATTER:

½ C. Crisco	2¼ C. flour
1½ C. sugar	3 tsp. baking powder
3 eggs	½ tsp. salt
1 tsp. vanilla	1 C. milk

Grease 9×12-inch pan. Sprinkle 1 C. miniature marshmallows on bottom. Pour batter over marshmallows. Add strawberries on top. Bake 25 minutes at 350°.

Burnt Sugar Cake

Brown ½ C. sugar   *Add ¼ C. water*

Let come to a light brown color. Cool.

1½ C. sugar   1 C. cold water
½ C. butter (or shortening)   2 C. flour
2 egg yolks   2 tsp. baking powder

Cream sugar, butter; add egg yolks, 1 C. cold water, 2 C. flour. Beat 5 minutes. Add 2 tsp. baking powder, ½ C. flour, 2 stiffly beat egg whites, burnt sugar and 1 tsp. vanilla. Fold in. Bake at 350° for 30-35 minutes.

Strawberry Cake

1 box white cake mix   *½ pkg. frozen strawberries*
⅓ C. melted shortening   *½ C. cold water*

Beat above ingredients 2 minutes, then add 4 unbeaten egg whites. Beat with electric mixer for 5 minutes. Bake 30 minutes at 350° Use 9 × 13-inch glass baking dish.

FROSTING:
1 box powdered sugar   1-2 drops red coloring
½ C. drained frozen strawberries   ½ tsp. vanilla
½ C. melted oleo (not hot)

Cool cake thoroughly before frosting.

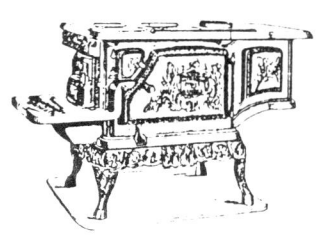

Pear Bran Muffins

1 C. flour	*1 (16 oz.) can pears in natural*
½ C. sugar	*juices*
2½ tsp. baking powder	*½ C. milk*
½ tsp. salt	*¼ C. oil*
1¼ C. whole bran cereal	*1 egg (beaten)*

Combine flour, sugar, baking powder and salt. Drain and dice pears; combine with bran and milk. Let stand 5 minutes. Add oil and egg to pear mixture; add all at once to flour mixture. Stir only until dry ingredients are moistened. Fill greased muffin pans ¾ full. Bake at 400° for 18-20 minutes or until wooden pick inserted near center comes out clean. Makes 1 dozen.

Muffins

2 C. boiling water	*2 C. Nabisco 100% Bran*

Let soak. While soaking mix below ingredients:

1 C. Crisco	*3 C. white sugar*
4 eggs	*1 qt. buttermilk*

SIFT:

5 C. flour	*5 tsp. soda*
1 tsp. salt	

Mix above ingredients, Nabisco 100% bran mixture and add 5 C. Kellogg's All Bran. Bake 20 minutes at 350° or spoon in bowl (small) for microwave (approximately 45 seconds). Yield 4 qts. Store in refrigerator and use as desired.

Refrig Coffee Cake

¾ C. oleo   1 C. white sugar
½ C. brown sugar   2 eggs

SIFT:
2 C. flour   1 tsp. baking powder
1 tsp. soda   1 tsp. nutmeg
½ tsp. salt

TOPPING:
½ C. brown sugar   1 tsp. cinnamon

Cream shortening, sugars and eggs. Sift dry ingredients together. Mix with creamed mixture. Add 1 C. of sour cream, also 1 C. of nuts, if desired. Pour into 9 × 13-inch greased pan. Sprinkle brown sugar and cinnamon over the top. Cover and refrigerate overnight. The next morning, preheat oven to 350° and bake for 35-40 minutes.

Cheesecake

1 (3 oz.) pkg. lemon Jello   28 graham cracker squares
1 (8 oz.) pkg. cream cheese   1 T. powdered sugar
1 (13 oz.) can evaporated milk   1 stick oleo or butter
1 C. sugar   ½ C. nuts
1 tsp. vanilla

Combine graham cracker crumbs, rolled fine with the powdered sugar and oleo. Save some crumbs for the topping. Pat into 9 × 13-inch pan and bake at 350° for 5-8 minutes. Mix lemon Jello with 1 C. boiling water. Cool until slightly jelled. Beat together cream cheese, sugar and vanilla. Add cooled Jello. Beat evaporated milk until consistency of whipped cream. Mix into cream cheese with spatula. Pour over crust and top with graham crackers and nuts.

Sour Cream Coffee Cake

½ C. margarine
1 C. sugar
2 eggs
2 C. flour
1 tsp. baking powder

1 tsp. soda
½ tsp. salt
1 C. sour cream
1 tsp. vanilla

TOPPING:
⅓ C. brown sugar
¼ C. white sugar

1 T. cinnamon
1 C. chopped nuts

Cream margarine and sugar well. Add eggs, 1 at a time and beat well. Sift together flour, baking powder, soda and salt; add alternately with sour cream and vanilla. Pour half of batter in greased Bundt pan. Combine topping ingredients. Sprinkle half of topping over batter. Pour rest of batter in pan. Top with remaining topping. Bake at 325° for 40-45 minutes.

DESSERTS

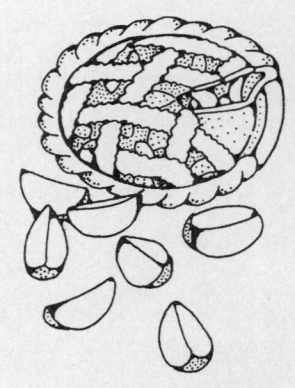

Desserts

Desserts - Continued

Desserts - Continued

Oatmeal Pie

3 eggs (beaten)
⅔ C. white sugar
1 C. brown sugar
2 T. butter
⅔ C. coconut

⅔ C. oatmeal
1 tsp. vanilla
¼ C. nutmeats (pecans preferred)
Unbaked pie shell

Beat eggs, sugar, butter and vanilla together. Add coconut and oatmeal. Put in unbaked pie shell. Sprinkle with nutmeat. Bake at 350° for 35 minutes.

Crustless Crab Quiche

½ lb. fresh mushrooms (thinly sliced)
2 T. butter or margarine
4 eggs
½ pt. (1 C.) sour cream
1 C. small curd cottage cheese
4 T. flour
½ C. Parmesan cheese

1 tsp. onion powder
¼ tsp. salt
4 drops Tabasco sauce
2 C. shredded Monterey Jack cheese (½ lb.)
6 oz. fresh or frozen crabmeat (thawed and well drained)

Preheat oven to 350°. Saute mushrooms in butter or margarine until tender. Remove mushrooms with a slotted spoon and drain on paper towels. In a blender, blend eggs, sour cream, cottage cheese, Parmesan cheese, flour, onion powder, salt and Tabasco sauce. Pour mixture in large bowl. Stir in sauteed mushrooms, Jack cheese and crabmeat. our into a 10-inch porcelain quiche dish or a 9½-inch deep dish pie plate. Bake 45 minutes or until knife inserted near center comes out clean. Quiche should be puffed and browned. Let stand 5 minutes before cutting into wedges. Serves 6. (VARIATION: Substitute ½ lb. cooked ham for crabmeat.)

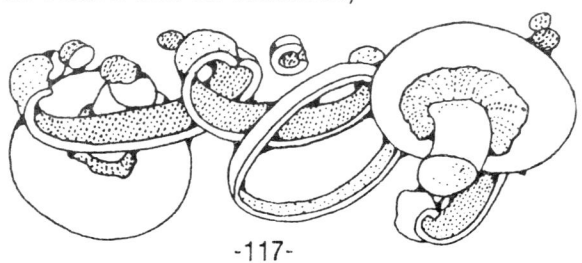

Tapioca Pudding

3 eggs (separated)
1 C. sugar
1 qt. milk

¼ C. tapioca (heaping)
1 tsp. vanilla

Mix and boil 3 egg yolks (beaten), sugar, milk and tapioca. Beat egg whites stiff and add to mixture. Remove from heat and add vanilla; stir well.

Rhubarb Dessert

1½ C. flour
7 T. powdered sugar
¾ C. oleo
2½ C. sugar
¼ C. flour

1 tsp. vanilla
3 beaten eggs
Dash of salt
1 C. evaporated milk

Crumb flour, powdered sugar and oleo; pat in ungreased 9 × 13-inch pan. Bake at 325° for 15 minutes. Sprinkle 4 C. or more rhubarb on hot crust. Then pour over the rest of the ingredients. Bake at 325° for 45-60 minutes.

Apple Crisp

1 C. flour	*¼ tsp. salt*
½ C. brown sugar	*4 T. water*
⅔ C. white sugar	*10-12 tart apples*
½ C. butter	*Little cinnamon*

Mix butter, brown sugar, flour and salt to form crumbly mixture. Butter baking dish and fill ¾ full of sliced apples mixed with white sugar, cinnamon and water. Cover with crumbled mixture and bake at 350° about 45 minutes. Serve with whipped cream.

Cocoa Ripple Ring

½ C. shortening	*1 .C sugar (divided)*
2 eggs	*1½ C. all-purpose flour*
¾ tsp. salt	*2 tsp. baking powder*
⅔ C. milk	*⅓ C. cocoa*
⅓ C. chopped nuts	*3 T. butter (softened)*

Cream shortening, ¾ C. sugar and eggs until light and fluffy. Sift together flour, salt and baking powder; add to creamed mixture alternately with milk, beating well after each addition. Spoon ⅓ of batter into a well-greased 6½ C. ring mold or round 9-inch cake pan. Combine remaining ¼ C. sugar, cocoa and nuts; sprinkle half over batter in pan and dot with half of butter. Repeat layers and top with remaining third of batter. Bake at 350° for 35 minutes or til done. Let stand for 5 minutes, turn out of mold and serve hot.

Pumpkin Roll

3 eggs
1 C. sugar
⅔ C. pumpkin
1 tsp. lemon juice
¾ C. flour
1 tsp. baking powder

2 tsp. cinnamon
1½ tsp. ginger
½ tsp. nutmeg
½ tsp. salt
1 C. chopped nuts (opt.)

FILLING:
1 C. powdered sugar
2 (3 oz. ea.) pkg. cream cheese

4 tsp. margarine
½ tsp. vanilla

Beat eggs for 5 minutes, gradually beating in sugar. Stir in pumpkin and lemon juice. Stir together flour, baking powder, cinnamon, ginger, nutmeg and salt. Fold into first mixture. Spread in greased and lightly floured jelly roll pan. Top with nuts and bake at 375° for 15 minutes. Immediately turn out on towel dusted with powdered sugar. Starting at narrow end, roll the towel. Cool. Unroll. For Filling: Combine powdered sugar, cream cheese, margarine and vanilla. Beat until smooth. Spread on roll; roll up and store in refrigerator.

Fruit Cobbler

2 large cans fruit (peaches, pears,
   apples or apricots)
1 C. flour
1 C. sugar
1 tsp. baking powder

½ tsp. salt
1 egg
½ C. melted butter
1 tsp. cinnamon or nutmeg

Put fruit in 9 x 13-inch pan. Mix flour, sugar, baking powder and salt. Mix well. Break one egg (unbeaten) into the mixture, mix until crumbly. Sprinkle over the fruit. Melt butter and pour over the top. Sprinkle cinnamon or nutmeg over all. Bake at 350° for 1½ hours.

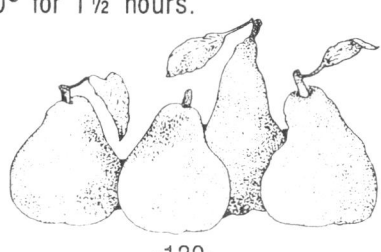

Vanilla Wafer Dessert

2 C. crushed vanilla wafers
1 stick oleo (melted)
2 eggs
2 sticks oleo
3½ C. powdered sugar
1 tsp. vanilla

5 medium bananas
1 large can crushed pineapple
Cool Whip
Chopped pecans
Marachino cherries

Mix together wafers, melted oleo and press into pan. Beat for 5 minutes the 2 eggs, 2 sticks oleo, powdered sugar and vanilla. Spread over vanilla wafers. Slice and spread 5 medium bananas over above ingredients. Spread large can of crushed pineapple (drained) over all. Top with a large container of Cool Whip. Garnish with chopped pecans and maraschino cherries. Refrigerate overnight.

Cherry Slices

½ C. brown sugar
20 graham crackers (rolled fine)
½ C. melted butter
2 T. flour
1 can Bordens cond. milk

2 C. coconut
2 C. powdered sugar
2 T. Half & Half
Cherries

Mix brown sugar, graham crackers, butter and flour. Bake in 8 × 8-inch pan at 275° for 8 minutes. Mix milk and coconut; pour over crust. Bake at 300° for 25 minutes. Cool and ice with mixture of powdered sugar, Half & Half, cherry juice and some cut-up cherries for color. Use either almond or lemon extract for flavoring.

Strawberry Spring Delight

1 large angel food cake
2 (3 oz. ea.) boxes instant vanilla
  pudding
2 C. milk
1 qt. vanilla ice cream

3 boxes strawberry Jello
3 C. hot water
2 (10 oz. ea.) pkgs. frozen
  strawberries

Break cake in pieces in 9 × 13-inch pan. Mix pudding, milk and ice cream together and put over the cake; let chill. Mix Jello, water and strawberries and let thicken. Pour over the pudding and refrigerate.

Banana Split Dessert

3 C. crushed graham crackers
2 sticks oleo
2 C. sugar
2 eggs
1 tsp. vanilla
Bananas
Nuts

Miniature chocolate chips
1 can crushed pineapple (drained)
1 large container Cool Whip
Maraschino cherries (drained and
  halved)
Sliced strawberries

Melt one stick oleo and combine with graham crackers. Pat into 11 × 13-inch pan. Mix 1 stick oleo, sugar, eggs and vanilla with blender or electric mixer for 10 minutes. Spread over graham cracker crust. Sprinkle with chips. Layer pineapple, bananas and strawberries. Cover with Cool Whip. Top with chopped pecans and cherries. Refrigerate overnight for easier cutting and serving.

Ice Cream (Without Cream)

6 eggs (well-beaten)   1 can Carnation milk
2 C. sugar   4 T. vanilla
2 (½ pts.) Richs whipped topping

Pour in ice cream container and add milk as needed to fill. Pack with salt and ice and freeze in ice cream freezer. Makes 1 gallon.

Cherry-Coconut Dessert

1 can Wilderness cherries   2 sticks margarin (melted)
1 small can chunk pineapple   ½ C. nuts
   (drained)   1 C. coconut
1 box yellow cake mix

Put cherry pie filling in 9 x 13-inch buttered pan; add drained pineapple, then the cake mix. Cover with melted margarine, then the nuts. Bake in 350° oven for 45 minutes, then add 1 C. flaked coconut. Bake another 15 minutes. serve with whipped cream.

Cherry Cobbler

2 C. flour   1⅓ C. milk
2 C. sugar   3 C. fresh cherries
4 tsp. (level) baking powder   1¼ C. sugar
Dash salt

Mix first 5 ingredients and pour in a greased 9 x 13-inch pan. Pour cherries on top of this. Sprinkle sugar over cherries. Bake at 325° for 45-55 minutes. Serve with ice cream.

Strawberry Graham Cracker Dessert

15 graham crackers
¼ C. sugar
½ C. milk
¼ C. melted butter

½ C. chopped nuts (opt.)
½ lb. marshmallows
1 C. whipping cream
1 pt. sweetened strawberries (2 C.)

Roll graham crackers fine and add melted butter and sugar. Mix well and pat into greased baking dish. Reserve 2 T. cracker crumbs for top. Melt marshmallows in top of double boiler with milk. Cool this mixture. Add cream which has been whipped. Place layer of marshmallow mixture in dish and then the strawberries and nuts mixed lightly together. Add remaining marshmallow mixture and top with reserved cracker crumbs.

Marshmallow Dessert

30 large marshmallows
½ or ¾ C. pineapple
1 C. milk

½ pt. cream
14 graham crackers (crushed fine)

Dissolve marshmallows in milk in a double boiler. Set aside to cool. Whip the cream. Roll cracker crumbs fine and put half in bottom of 9×13-inch pan. Drain pineapple and add to marshmallows and milk. Fold in whipped cream. Spoon the mixture on the crumbs and sprinkle balance of crumbs on top. Place in refrigerator for about 8 hours so as to serve cold.

Sherbet Macaroon Dessert

18 coconut macaroons (crumbled)
1 C. chopped nuts
½ C. chopped maraschino cherries
   (opt.)
2 pkgs. prepared Dream Whip

½ gal. rainbow sherbet or 1 pt.
   each lime, pineapple, orange or
   lemon sherbet (using just ½ gal.
   raspberrry sherbet is also good)

Combine macaroon crumbs, nuts and cherries (opt.). Prepare Dream Whip according to package directions and add to macaroon mixture. Spread ½ of mixture in 9×13-inch pan. Spoon sherbet over this and stir to give marble effect. Cover with remaining macaroon mixture. Remove 15 minutes before serving.

Pineapple Dessert

16 graham crackers (crushed)
1 C. sugar
½ C. soft butter
2 eggs (separated)

1 C. drained crushed pineapple
¾ C. nuts
2 boxes cherry Jello

Layer graham cracker crumbs in cake pan. Cream together sugar, butter and 2 egg yolks. Add pineapple and nuts. Beat 2 egg whites until stiff and fold in mixture. Pour into cake pan. Prepare Jello as directed on package and when it starts to set, pour evenly in cake pan. Refrigerate until set.

Ice Cream Delight

½ gal. soft ice cream (any flavor)
2 C. Rice Chex (crushed)
1 C. shredded coconut

½ C. chopped nuts
⅔ C. brown sugar
⅓ C. melted butter

Mix well, all but the ice cream. Put ⅔ mixture on bottom of 8×12-inch pan. Then put the ice cream on the top. Next add the remaining ⅓ mixture. Put in freezer.

Curried Fruit Cake

1 (No. 2) can pear halves
1 (No. 2) can peach halves
1 (No. 2) can apricot halves
1 (No. 2) can pineapple spears
  (cut up)

1 small jar maraschino cherries
¾ C. brown sugar
½ C. melted butter
Dash of curry powder
¼ C. apricot brandy

Drain all fruits and arrange in casserole or flat baking dish. Mix together curry powder, brown sugar and butter. Pour over fruit and bake 1 hour in 325° oven. Dish can be left in oven (turned off) for 2-3 hours. Good served with ham or chicken.

Apple Dessert

2 qts. slices apples
2 C. sugar
2 T. flour
1 tsp. cinnamon
2 C. oatmeal

2 C. flour
2 C. brown sugar
½ tsp. soda
1 tsp. baking powder
5 T. melted oleo or butter

Combine first 4 ingredients, mix good and put in greased pan or dish. Mix remaining ingredients together in dish and put over apple mixture. Bake at 350° for 30-40 minutes in 9×13-inch pan, greased. Serves 12.

Strawberry Dessert

1 C. flour
¼ C. brown sugar
½ C. chopped nuts
¼ C. melted oleo
2 egg whites

⅔ C. sugar
2 T. lemon juice
1 (10 oz.) pkg. strawberries
   (partly thawed)
Dream Whip

Mix first 4 ingredients together and spread evenly in 9 × 13-inch cake pan. Bake at 350° for 20 minutes, stirring every 5 minutes while in oven. Cool. Spread ⅔ in pan and save rest for top. Next, beat egg whites, sugar, lemon juice until very thick. Fold into egg mixture the thawed strawberries until well blended. Fold in 2 pkgs. Dream Whip (whip before starting the recipe). Freeze and serve directly from the freezer.

Yellow Cake Dessert

1 yellow cake mix
1 (20 oz.) can crushed pineapple
½ C. sugar

1 box instant vanilla pudding
½ C. coconut
1 (8 oz.) tub whipped topping

Bake cake as directed on box. Remove from oven and punch holes in cake with meat fork over entire top about every inch. While cake is baking, heat pineapple and sugar until sugar is dissolved. Pour this while hot, juice and all, over the top of the hot cake. Then cool. After cake is cool, prepare the pudding. Add coconut and spread immediately over the top of pineapple. After pudding is set, put whipped topping over the top of cake. Keep in refrigerator.

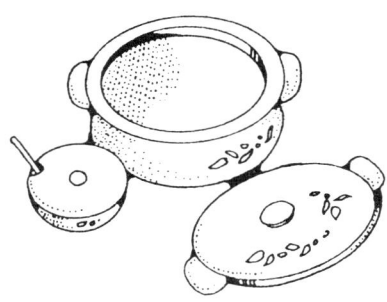

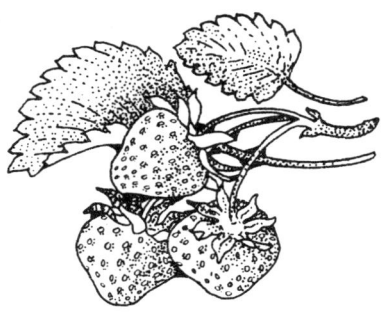

Lori's Dessert

1 lb. marshmallows
½ C. milk
2 C. cream (whipped) or 2 pkgs.
  Dream Whip
Oreo or Hydrox cookies

½ C. black walnuts
1 small can crushed pineapple or
  strawberries (fresh or frozen)
  (If frozen strawberries, add
  sugar)

Crush cookies and line bottom of 9×13-inch pan. Save small amount for topping. Melt marshmallows and milk together (in double boiler or microwave). Let cool. When cooled thoroughly, add whipped cream, fruit and nuts. Cover crushed cookies with above cooled mixture. Cover with remaining crushed cookies. Chill in refrigerator 6-8 hours before serving. (This is especially good when made with strawberries.)

Oreo Dessert

1 small pkg. Oreos (crushed; 42)
½ gal. softened mint ice cream
8 oz. Cool Whip

1 jar Smuckers chocolate fudge
  topping

Crush cookies, put into 9×13-inch pan; pat down. Freeze 20 minutes. Put ice cream on top. Freeze 20 minutes. Spread chocolate fudge on top. Freeze 20 minutes. Coyer with Cool Whip.

Lime Dessert

1 pkg. lime Jello	1 small can crushed pineapple
1¼ C. boiling water	½ C. chopped nuts
2 egg whites	1 container Cool Whip
¼ C. sugar	Crushed graham crackers

Dissolve Jello in boiling water. Beat egg whites till stiff and beat in sugar. Fold quickly in boiling Jello - folding till all the whites are pale green. Add entire can of crushed pineapple. Pour into square pan and chill till firm. When ready to serve, sprinkle chopped nuts on top and cover with Cool Whip. Crush a few graham crackers and spread over top. Cut in sqaures. Any flavor of Jello maybe used.

Four Layer Dessert

1 C. flour	1 C. Cool Whip
¼ C. brown sugar (packed)	1 large pkg. strawberry Jello
½ C. margarine	1 lb. frozen strawberries
½ C. nuts	2 C. boiling water
1 (8 oz.) pkg. cream cheese	1 C. Cool Whip
(softened)	½ C. chopped nuts
1 C. powdered sugar	

Combine flour, brown sugar, margarine and nuts with fingers. Press in 9 × 13-inch pan and bake at 350° for 15 minutes; cool. Combine cream cheese, powdered sugar and Cool Whip. Spread on first layer. Combine Jello, strawberries and boiling water. Mix and chill. When it is beginning to thicken, pour over second layer in pan and chill. Top last layer with Cool Whip and nuts I also use raspberries with raspberry Jello.

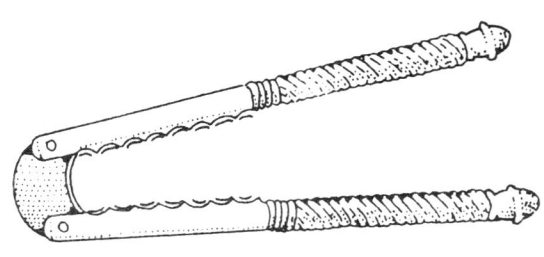

Cherry Dessert

1¼ C. flour
½ C. sugar
⅔ C. margarine
½ C. nuts (opt.)
1 (8 oz.) pkg. cream cheese
1 C. powdered sugar
1 C. whipped topping

5 C. pitted cherries (can use home grown)
3 T. tapioca
3 T. cornstarch
1¼ C. sugar
1 tub whipped topping

Mix flour, sugar, margarine and nuts together and pat in bottom of 9 x 13-inch pan and bake 15 minutes. Brown very slightly in 350° oven. Mix cream cheese, sugar and topping together well and spread over cooled crust. Mix cherries and tapioca together and let set 10 minutes. Then put on medium heat, when it starts to bubble, add the cornstarch and sugar. Simmer and stir until nice and thick. Cool well before putting over the cream cheese layer. Cover cherry mixture with a whipped topping. Keep in refrigerator.

Pineapple-Coconut Torte

1 pt. whipping cream or 1 pkg.
   Dream Whip (whipped)
4 egg whites
1 C. sugar

1 T. Knox gelatin
1 (No. 303) size can crushed
   pineapple
1 pkg. coconut cookies

Beat egg whites stiff, add sugar gradually. Add well drained pineapple. Dissolve gelatin in a little cold water, add enough hot water to make ½ C. Whip cream stiff, add. Crush part of cookies, line pan. Pour half of mixture, then lay whole cookies in a layer. Finish with rest of pineapple mixture. Sprinkle crushed cookies over top.

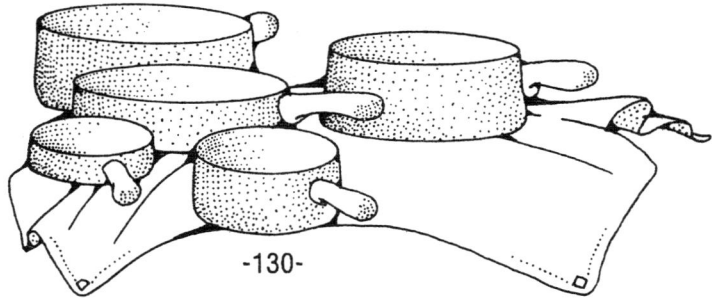

Cherry Dessert

1 (16-18) pkg. graham crackers (crushed)
½ C. melted butter
¼ C. sugar

1 pkg. powdered whipped cream
1 C. powdered sugar
1 (3 oz.) pkg. cream cheese
1 can cherry pie filling

Crush graham crackers, mix in butter and sugar. Place in 9 x 9-inch pan. Second layer: whip cream, add powdered sugar, cream cheese. Whip together and spread over graham crackers. Spread on top the can of cherry pie filling. Chill overnight before serving.

Rhubarb Crisp

4 C. cut rhubarb
1¼ C. sugar
½ tsp. cinnamon
1 T. flour
¾ C. flour

½ C. oatmeal
½ C. packed brown sugar
½ C. margarine
Salt

Place rhubarb in shallow pan. Combine sugar, flour and cinnamon. Sprinkle over fruit. For Topping: Mix ¾ C. flour, brown sugar and a dash of salt. Cut in margarine and stir in oatmeal. Sprinkle over fruit and bake at 350° for 1 hour. Makes 8 servings. 345 calories.

Cherry Dessert

2 C. vanilla wafers (crushed)
¼ C. butter (melted)
1½ C. powdered sugar
8 oz. pkg. Phil. cream cheese

½ pt. cream (whipped)
1 can cherry pie filling
½ C. sugar
2 T. cherry Jello mix

Combine vanilla wafers and butter. Press into bottom of square pan for crust. Mix well the powdered sugar and cream cheese. Add the cream and pour over crust. Heat cherry pie filling with sugar and cherry Jello. When cool, pour over second layer and chill.

Ice Cream Dessert

⅓ C. butter
2¾ C. graham crackers
1½ qts. vanilla ice cream
½ C. butter

1½ C. powdered sugar
3 eggs (beaten)
2 sq. chocolate

Mix butter and crumbs; pat on bottom of 9×9-inch pan. Save some for topping. Cream butter and powdered sugar; add beaten eggs. Add 2 sq. of chocolate which have been melted. Mix and pour over crumb mixture. Put in freezer to set, then spread soften ice cream over chocolate mixture. Add remaining crumb topping, then freeze. Add nuts to top, if you like.

Clara's Rhubarb Torte

3 C. diced rhubarb
1 C. sifted flour
1 C. sugar
¾ T. salt

1 unbeaten egg
½ C. shortening
1 tsp. baking powder

Place rhubarb in square pan. Put ½ C. sugar over rhubarb. Mix flour, ½ C. sugar, salt, egg, shortening and baking powder; sprinkle over rhubarb. Bake in moderate oven.

Rhubarb Dessert

Rhubarb
1½ C. sugar
2 (3 oz. ea.) boxes Jello
  (strawberry, raspberry or cherry)

1½ C. flour
½ C. powdered sugar
¾ C. butter

In a 9×9-inch pan, cut up rhubarb to fill the pan ¾ full. Mix the sugar and Jello together and mix in the rhubarb well. Mix the flour, powdered sugar adn butter until crumbly, then sprinkle on top of the rhubarb mixture, evenly. Bake at 350° for 30 minutes. Serve with Cool Whip or other whipped topping.

Peach Delight

29 oz. can sliced peaches
1 yellow box cake or butter
  brickle mix

1 stick margarine
1 C. sliced almonds

In a greased 9×13-inch pan, pour entire contents of sliced peaches and juice. Next pour over peaches the dry cake mix. Melt 1 stick margarine and dribble over cake mix. Top with sliced almonds. Bake at 325° for 50 minutes. Serve with ice cream or Cool Whip.

Coconut Pie

1 (9-inch) unbaked pie crust
3 eggs
1 T. flour
¾ C. sugar

1 C. light corn syrup
2 T. margarine (melted)
1 tsp. vanilla
1½ C. coconut

Beat eggs, sugar and flour. Add syrup and melted margarine and beat. Add vanilla and beat. Sprinkle coconut over bottom of unbaked pie crust. Pour the mixture over the coconut. Bake in slow oven (325°) for 40-45 minutes or until firm.

Jello Pudding Roll

3 eggs
1 C. sugar
¼ C. cold water
1 tsp. vanilla
1 C. sifted all-purpose flour

2 tsp. baking powder
½ tsp. salt
1 pkg. lemon Jello pudding
½ C. sugar
1 egg

Beat eggs until thick and lemon colored (5 minutes). Add sugar gradually, continuing to beat until light and fluffy. Add water and vanilla. Add sifted dry ingredients and blend until smooth. Pour into greased wax paper lined 15-inch jelly roll pan. Bake at 375° for 12-15 minutes. Turn out immediately onto tea towel, sprinkled with powdered sugar. Remove waxed paper. Trim any rough edges and roll cake up in cloth and place on rack to cool. Mix contents of Jello package and ½ C. sugar, substitute 1 whole egg for 2 egg yolks as indicated on package. Prepare as directed; cool. Unroll cake and spread on cooled filling. Roll up again and chill until ready to serve.

Lemon Dessert

1 stick oleo
1 C. flour
½ C. chopped pecans
1 (8 oz.) pkg. cream cheese
1 C. powdered sugar

1 C. Cool Whip
2 small pkgs. instant lemon
   pudding mix
3 C. milk
½ C. ground pecans

Mix well the oleo, flour and pecans; pat into a 9 × 13-inch pan. Bake at 350° for 15 minutes; cool. Combine cream cheese, powdered sugar, Cool Whip and spread on first layer. Mix lemon pudding mix with milk. Beat well and pour over second layer. Cover with rest of Cool Whip and sprinkle with ground pecans. Any flavor of pudding can be used.

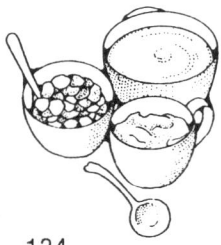

Banana Split Dessert

2 or 3 bananas
½ gal. Neopolitan ice cream
1 C. chopped walnuts
1 C. chocolate chips
Graham cracker crumbs

½ C. butter
2 C. powdered sugar
1½ C. evaporated milk
1 tsp. vanilla
1 pt. whipping cream

Cover bottom of 11 × 15-inch pan with a graham cracker crust. Reserve 1 cup crumbs. Slice bananas cross-wise and layer over crust. Slice ice cream in ½-inch thick slices and place over bananas. Sprinkle ice cream with chopped nuts. Freeze until firm. Melt chocolate chips and butter. Add powdered sugar and evaporated milk. Cook mixture until thick and smooth, stirring constantly. Remove from heat and add vanilla. Cool chocolate mixture, then pour over ice cream. Freeze until firm. Whip cream until stiff. Spread over chocolate layer and top with reserved crumbs. Store in freezer. Remove about 10 minutes before serving. Will keep for serveral weeks. Makes about 25 servings.

Apple Bread Pudding

9-12 slices firm white bread (cut into halves)
2 C. Half and Half (light cream)
½ C. each sugar and water
½ tsp. vanilla

6-8 medium sized apples (peeled, cored and sliced)
2 eggs
½ tsp. ground cinnamon
2 tsp. butter/margarine
Cream (opt.)

(Leftover bread may be used for this recipe.) Place bread slices in a single layer in a shallow pan. Pour evenly ½ C. of Half and Half over the bread. In a saucepan bring to a boil the sugar and water. Reduce heat and simmer 5 minutes. Stir in vanila and add ⅓ of the apple slices, a dn simmer each portion 3 minutes. Remove the apples with a slotted spoon reserving the sugar syrup. In a buttered 2½-qt. baking dish, line the bottom with ⅓ of the bread slices. Top with half of the apples. Make a layer of another ⅓ of the bread. Cover with the rest of the apples, covering with the rest of the bread. Beat eggs slightly; mix in cinnamon, then the remaining 1½ C. Half and Half and the sugar syrup from the apples. Pour this mixture over the bread and apples. Dot with butter or margarine. Bake at 350° until top layer is brown and crusty, about 1 hour. Serve hot or at room temperature, with cream if you desire.

Apple Dumplings

SYRUP:
2 C. sugar
2 C. water
¼ tsp. cinnamon

¼ tsp. nutmeg
¼ C. butter or margarine

DOUGH:
2 C. flour
1 tsp. salt
2 tsp. baking powder

¾ C. shortening
½ C. milk

Make syrup of sugar, water, cinnnamon and nutmeg; add butter. Pare and core apples, cut into fourths. Sift flour, salt and baking powder. Cut in shortening. Add milk all at once and stir until moistened. Roll ¼-inch thick, cut into 5-inch squares. Arrange 4 pieces of apple on each square, sprinkle generously with additional sugar, cinnamon and nutmeg, dot with butter. Fold corners to center, pinch edges together. Place 1-inch apart in greased baking pan about 9 × 13-inch pan. Pour syrup over them. Bake in moderate oven, 375°, about 35 minutes. Makes 8 dumplings.

Ann's Pie Crust

3 C. flour
1 tsp. salt
1 C. shortening

1 egg (beaten)
⅓ C. water
1 tsp. vinegar

Blend flour, salt and shortening together. Stir in egg and liquid; roll. Can be rerolled without getting tough. Makes three 9-inch pie shells.

Coconut Crunch Pudding

CRUNCH:
1 C. flour
¼ C. brown sugar

½ C. soft butter
1 C. coconut

1 pkg. vanilla pudding mix
2 C. milk
Pinch of salt
3 eggs (separated)

2 T. butter
1 tsp. vanilla
½ tsp. banana flavoring
2-3 bananas

For Crunch: Mix flour and brown sugar, cut in butter and mix until crumbly. Add coconut and mix until blended.

Mix pudding mix, salt, milk and egg yolks. Cook as directed on package. Add butter, vanilla and banana flavoring. Beat egg whites with the ¼ C. sugar and fold into cooked pudding. Layer into the pan, first crunch, then pudding, bananas, pudding, bananas, and end with crunch.

Apple Turnovers

3 C. flour
3 T. sugar
1½ tsp. salt
½ tsp. cinnamon

1¾ C. Crisco
1 (20-22 oz.) can prepared apple
    pie filling
Confectioner's sugar

(NOTE: Any prepared pie filling may used.) Preheat oven to 425°. Combine flour, granulated sugar, salt, cinnamon. Cut in Crisco with pastry blender or two knives until mixture is uniform. Sprinkle dough with water a tablespoon at a time, stirring it with a fork until just enough has been added so dough can be patted into a ball. Divide pastry in half. On a lightly floured surface, roll ½ itno a 10×15-inch rectangle. Cut into six 5-inch squares. Repeat with other half of dough. Place about 2 measuring tablespoons of fruit in center of each square. Moisten pastry edges with water. Fold over ½ pastry to form triangle. Seal edges firmly with a fork. Prick top with a fork for steam to escape. Bake on ungreased baking sheet 12-15 minutes or until lightly browned. Cool slightly. Sprinkle with confectioner's sugar. Makes 12.

Dessert Bread Pudding

¾ C. (or less) brown sugar
3 slices bread (cubed)
3 eggs (beaten)
1½ C. milk

½ tsp. vanilla
½ tsp. cinnamon
½ C. raisins

Put brown sugar in bottom of greased double boiler. Add bread cubes. Don't stir. Add raisins. Beat eggs with milk and pour over mixture. Do not stir or peek. Cook for 1 hour with lid on. Keep water boiling.

Alice's Lemon Pudding

1 C. sugar
1 T. butter
1 lemon (juice & rind)

2 T. flour
2 eggs
1 C. milk

Cream 1 C. sugar with 1 T. butter. Add juice and rind of 1 lemon, 2 T. flour, yolks of 2 eggs, 1 C. milk and last add beaten whites of 2 eggs. Set in a pan of warm water until done, or for about 1 hour (350° oven).

Blueberry Desset

22 graham crackers
½ C. melted butter
¼ C. sugar

2 cans blueberry pie mix
2 C. whipping cream
1 (10 oz.) pkg. miniature
  marshmallows

Mix well the graham crackers, melted butter and sugar for crust. Put half of crust in bottom of pan. Whip cream and add marshmallows. Place half on top of crust. Add blueberry pie mix to next layer, whipped cream to next layer, and top with remaining graham crackers. Can be frozen.

Rice Cream

1 qt. whipping cream
2 T. plain gelatin
2½ C. boiled rice
½ C. sugar

½ tsp. almond flavoring
Chopped almonds
Pieces of pineapple
Red raspberry sauce

Dissolve gelatin in a little cold water. Cook rice. After rice is cool, add stiffly beaten cream and gelatin, chopped almonds or pieces of pineapple or both. Served with red raspberry sauce.

Baked Custard

6 eggs
¾ C. sugar
½ tsp. salt

4 C. scalded milk
½ tsp. vanilla
Nutmeg, as desired

Beat eggs; add sugar and salt, mixing well. Add milk, scalded or not and vanilla. Bake at 350° to 375° for 1 to 1½ hours, depending on depth of baking dish. Place baking dish in larger pan that has 1-1½ inch of hot water in it, to bake.

Old Fashioned Bread Pudding

8 slices of bread (broken up)
1 C. sugar
1 C. raisins

3 eggs
1 qt. milk
1 tsp. salt

Combine all ingredients and put in cake pan. Bake at 350° for 45 minutes or knife inserted 1-inch from edge comes out clean.

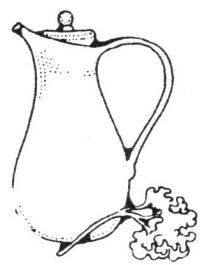

Rena's Coconut Pie

1 (9-inch) pie crust (unbaked)	½ tsp. salt
4 eggs or 8 egg yolks	⅔ C. milk or cream
⅔ C. sugar	1½ C. fresh toasted coconut

Mix eggs, sugar, salt and milk. Add 1 C. coconut and pour into crust. Bake on lowest oven rack at 400° for 15 minutes. Turn heat down to 350° for 25-30 minutes. The last 5-10 minutes, add the rest of the coconut.

Peach Cheese Dessert

1 C. + 2 T. flour	2 C. Cool Whip
1 C. chopped nuts	1½ C. water
¼ C. brown sugar	¼ C. sugar
1 stick margarine (melted)	2 T. cornstarch
8 oz. cream cheese	3 oz. peach Jello
½ C. powdered sugar	4 C. peaches (sliced)
1 tsp. vanilla	

Mix first 4 ingredients and press in 9 × 13-inch pan. Bake 15 minutes at 350°. Cool. Mix softened cheese, sugar, vanilla and Cool Whip. Spread over crust and chill. Cook water, sugar and cornstarch until thick. Add Jello and sliced peaches. Pour over and chill.

Pumpkin Dessert

2 C. pumpkin	2 tsp. nutmeg
1 C. sugar	1 C. pecans
1 tsp. salt	½ gal. vanilla ice cream
1 tsp. ginger	Gingersnaps
1 tsp. cinnamon	Whipped cream

Mix ingredients in order and fold in softened ice cream. Line bottom of pan with gingersnaps. Add ½ of mixture, then layer of gingersnaps. Freeze and garnish with whipped cream and pecans.

Baked Fruit

1 large can cling peaches
1 large can apricot halves
1 large can pineapple chunks
4 T. minute tapioca

3 T. brown sugar
Dash of cinnamon
Dash of nutmeg
Dot with butter

Drain the fruit. Mix fruit with tapioca. Put in casserole or baking dish. Sprinkle with sugar, cinnamon, nutmeg. Dot with butter. Bake 1 hour at 350°. *Double this recipe for a large crowd.

Buster Bar Dessert

1 (15 oz.) pkg. Oreo cookies
½ C. melted butter
½ gal. vanilla ice cream

1 (16 oz.) can Hershey's fudge
topping
9 oz. Cool Whip

Crush Oreos and reserve 1 C. crumbs. Add melted butter to the rest of crumbs and pat into 9 × 13-inch pan. Add ice cream that has been softened. Place in freezer. When frozen, spread fudge topping over ice cream. Cover with Cool Whip. Sprinkle with reserved crumbs and freeze.

Broccoli Pie

1 lb. hamburger
1 onion (chopped)
8 oz. Philadelphia cream cheese

8 oz. mozzarella cheese or Swiss cheese
1 can Pillsbury crescent dough
1 large box broccoli spears pieces

Cook broccoli in salt water and drain. Brown hamburger and onion. Spread dough in a pie pan to form a pie shell. Drain hamburger mixture and combine with broccoli and cream cheese. Pour in pie shell and bake at 350° for 25 minutes. Remove from oven and cover with mozzarella cheese. Bake until cheese is melted.

Dream Whip Pumpkin Pie

1 pkg. Dream Whip
½ C. milk
½ tsp. vanilla
½ C. milk

1 pkg. vanilla instant pudding
1 C. canned pumpkin
¾ tsp. pumpkin pie spice
1 baked pie shell

Mix Dream Whip and ½ C. milk and ½ tsp. vanilla. In second bowl, mix ⅔ C. milk and 1 pkg. vanilla instant pudding. Let stand until stiff. Mix the two, using 1 C. of the prepared Dream Whip with the pudding mixture. Mix for about 1 minute. Mix 1 C. canned pumpkin and ¾ tsp. pumpkin pie spice. Mix this with the first mixture and place in baked pie shell. Top with the remaining Dream Whip. Chill for 2 hours.

Cherry Cheese Pie

1 graham cracker crumb crust
1 (8 oz.) pkg. cream cheese
(softened)
1 (14 oz.) can sweetened condensed milk

⅓ C. lemon juice
1 tsp. vanilla
1 (21 oz.) can cherry pie filling

Makes one 9-inch pie. In large mixer bowl, beat cheese until fluffy. Gradually beat in sweetened condensed milk until smooth. Stir in lemon juice and vanilla. Pour into prepared crust. Chill 3 hours or until set. Top with pie filling.

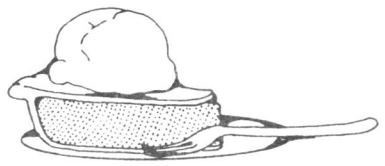

Sour Cream Raisin Pie

1 C. sour cream
1 C. sugar
1 egg
1 tsp. vinegar

1 tsp. cinnamon
½ tsp. cloves
1 C. raisins

Mix all ingredients thoroughly. Pour into unbaked 9-inch pie shell. Put top crust on, leaving vents for steam to escape. Bake at 350° until crust is lightly browned, about 45 minutes.

Pumpkin Pie

2 unbaked pie shells
2 C. pumpkin (cooked)
1 C. sugar
1-2 tsp. nutmeg
¾ tsp. cinnamon

½ tsp. allspice
½ tsp. salt
3 T. melted butter
3 eggs (slightly beaten)
2 C. milk (scalded)

Mix as given. Bake at 350° for 20 minutes. Reduce heat to 350° and finish baking. Sprinkle nutmeg over top when you put it in the oven.

Lemon Meringue Pie

1 C. sugar
3 T. Argo cornstarch
1½ C. cold water
3 egg yolks (slightly beaten)
1 lemon rind (grated)

¼ C. lemon juice
1 T. margarine
1 (9-inch) baked pastry shell
3 egg whites
⅓ C. sugar

Stir together 1 C. sugar and cornstarch in a 2 qt. saucepan. Gradually stir in water until smooth. Stir in beaten egg yolks, stirring constantly. Bring to boil over medium heat and boil for 1 minute. (Better to use a double boiler.) Remove from heat, stir in lemon rind, lemon juice and margarine; cool. Turn into pastry shell. Beat egg whites until foamy in small bowl with mixer at high speed. Add ⅓ C. sugar, 1 T. at a time, beating well after each addition. Continue beating until stiff peaks form. Spread some of meringue around edge of filling first, touching crust all around, then fill center. Bake at 350° for 15 minutes until lightly browned; cool. (The century was young, the horseless carriage was making a tentative appearance and ladies' skirts still swept the ground in the early 1900's when this classic recipe was printed on the Argo Cornstarch package. It is an easy-to-make lemon pie recipe which is also real good!)

Key Lime Pie

1 (9-inch) baked pastry shell
  (cooled)
1 (14 oz.) can cond. milk
  (not evap.)
A few drops of green food coloring
  (opt.)
⅓ C. sugar

4 eggs, separated (reserve 1 white
  for filling, 3 for meringue)
½ C. reconstituted lime juice
½ tsp. cream of tartar
Mint leaves (opt.)

Preheat oven to 350°. In medium bowl, beat egg yolks; stir in sweetened condensed milk, lime juice and food coloring. In small bowl, stiffly beat 1 egg white; fold into sweetened condensed milk mixture. Turn into shell. Beat remaining egg whites with cream of tartar until foamy; gradualy add sugar, beating until stiff but not dry. Spread meringue on top of pie; seal carefully to edge of shell. Bake for 12-15 minutes or until meringue is golden brown; cool. Chill before serving. If desired, garnish with mint leaves. Refrigerate leftovers.

Butterscotch Pie

1 C. brown sugar	2 beaten egg yolks
2 T. flour	2 T. butter
1 C. cold milk	1 tsp. vanilla
	Pinch of salt

Combine all ingredients in the order given. Place over heat and stir constantly until mixture thickens and is thoroughly cooked. Pour in baked pie crust and cover with meringue made of the two egg whites.

Cherry Pie

1 can drained cherries	2 egg yolks
1 T. flour	¼ C. cream
1 C. sugar	½ tsp. vanilla
¼ C. butter	

Put cherries in unbaked pie crust. Cream the butter, flour and sugar. Add egg yolks, beat until smooth. Add cream and vanilla. Pour this mixture over cherries. Place in hot oven, 450°, for 10 minutes. Reduce heat to 355° and bake for 30 minutes. Make meringue from egg whites and 2 T. sugar. Put on top of berry mixture and brown.

Super Pie

1 scant C. sugar
½ C. flour
2 C. milk
1 C. coconut

1 tsp. vanilla
1 stick margarine (melted)
4 eggs

Place in blender and mix well. Pour into a 9-inch buttered pie plate and bake at 350° for 40-50 minutes or until done.

Chocolate Angel Pie

2 egg whites
⅓ tsp. salt
1/8 tsp. cream of tartar
1 tsp. vanilla
1 C. (¼ lb.) Baker's sweetened choc.

3 T. hot water
1 tsp. vanilla
1 C. cream (whipped)
½ C. nutmeats

Beat egg whites until foamy. Add salt and cream of tartar. Beat until mixture stands very stiff. Fold in vanilla. Turn into light 8-inch pie plate. Makes a nest-like shell building sides up above plate. Bake in slow oven (300°) for 55 minutes. Cool. Melt chocolate in double boiler. Add hot water, blend and cool. Add vanilla. Fold in whipped cream; add nutmeats. Turn into the baked meringue shell and chill. Cover with whipped cream.

Chocolate Chip Pie

1 C. solid vegetable shortening	*½ tsp. baking soda*
½ C. firmly packed brown sugar	*1 tsp. salt*
½ C. sugar	*2 C. semi-sweet chocolate chips*
1 tsp. vanilla	*1 C. chopped walnuts*
2 eggs	*1 (9-inch) dish pie shell*
2 C. all-purpose flour	*Vanilla ice cream*
1 tsp. baking powder	

Preheat oven to 350°. Cream shortening, sugars and vanilla in a large mixing bowl, using electric mixer. Beat in 1 egg at a time. Combine flour, salt, soda and baking powder. Gradually blend in sugar mixture, stir in the walnuts and chocolate chips. Spoon into the pie shell, mounding slightly in the center. Bake until the top is slightly browned about 10 minutes. Reduced oven heat to 250°. Cover with foil. Bake until the center is desired firmness (about 1 hour for a chewy texture). Serve warm or at room temperature with the vanilla ice cream. Makes 6 or 8 servings.

Cherry Pie

2 (1 lb. ea.) cans water-packed red	*2 T. liquid sugar substitute*
tart cherries	*½ tsp. almond extract*
3 T cornstarch	*1 (9-inch) baked pie shell*

Drain cherries and pour juice into blender container. Add cornstarch and sugar substitute and blend for 20 seconds. Pour into saucepan, cook and stir over medium heat until thick, about 5 minutes. Cool to room temperature, add drained cherries, and flavoring. Pour into baked pie shell. Makes 6 servings, approximately 202 calories per serving.

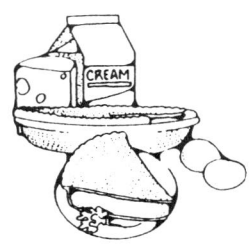

Peppermint Chiffon Pie

14 chocolate sandwich cookies
3 T. butter or margarine
1 env. unflavored gelatin
¾ C. finely crushed peppermint hard candy

1 C. milk
4 egg whites
2 T. sugar
1 C. heavy cream (whipped)

Crush cookies in plastic bag with rolling pin (makes about 1¼ C.). If fillings stick to inside a bag, scrape off with rubber spatula and blend with crumbs. Melt butter in medium-sized skillet; stir in cookie crumbs, remove from heat and stir for 1 minute. Press crumb mixture against sides and bottom of 9-inch pie plate. Chill while preparing filling. Sprinkle gelatin over milk in small heavy saucepan; let stand a few minutes to soften. Add ½ C. of the crushed candy. Cook, stirring constantly, over medium heat until gelatin is completely dissolved. Place pan in bowl of ice and water to speed setting; chill, stirring often, until mixture starts to thicken. While gelatin mixture chils, beat egg whites in medium-sized bowl until foamy white; gradually beat in sugar until meringue stands in soft peaks. Fold whipped cream, 2 T. of reserved crushed candy and meringue into gelatin mixture until no steaks of white remain; spoon into chilled ie crust. Chill for 4 hours or until firm.

Fudge Pie

1 (9-inch) unbaked pie shell
¼ C. butter
¾ C. brown sugar (packed)
3 eggs
2 C. chocolate chips

2 tsp. instant coffee
1 tsp. vanilla
¼ C. flour
1 C. chopped nuts
Whipped cream

Cream butter and brown sugar. Add eggs, 1 at a time. Beat well. Melt chocolate chips and add to above mixture. Stir in instant coffee, vanilla, flour and chopped nuts. Pour in unbaked pie shell. Bake at 375° for 25 minutes. Cool and top with whipped cream.

Georgia Peanut Butter Pie

1 baked 9-inch pie shell

BOTTOM LAYER:
1 C. powdered sugar   *⅓ C. creamy peanut butter*

FILLING:
¼ C. cornstarch   *2 C. scalded milk*
⅔ C. sugar   *3 egg yolks (beaten)*
¼ tsp. salt   *¼ tsp. vanilla*

TOPPING:
3 egg whites (beaten)

For Bottom Layer: Mix powdered sugar and peanut butter until like cornmeal. Spread ½ of this mixture in bottom of baked pie shell.

For Filling: Combine cornstarch, sugar, salt, scalded milk and beaten egg yolks. Cook until thick. Add vanilla and spread over peanut butter layer in pie crust.

For Topping: Beat egg whites. Spread over pie filling and sprinkle with rest of peanut butter mixture over egg whites. Bake until light brown, 20 minutes.

Apple Pie

6 C. sliced tart juicy apples   *¾ tsp. cinnamon*
¾ C. sugar   *1 T. butter*

Preheat oven to 425°. Combine apples, sugar and spice. Heap into pastry lined pie pan; dot with butter. Cover with top crust. Seal and flute edges. Bake at 425° for 50-60 minutes until done.

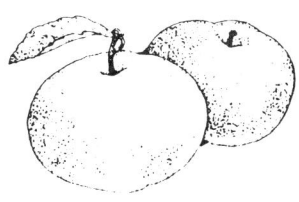

Sour Cream Raisin Pie

2 eggs (beaten)
1 C. granulated sugar
1 C. sour cream
1 T. flour
1 C. raisins
½ tsp. cinnamon

¼ tsp. cloves
1/8 tsp. nutmeg
¼ tsp. grated lemon rind
¼ tsp. salt
⅓ C. chopped nuts (opt.)
Pie shell

Add sugar and cream to eggs and beat thoroughly. Mix in the rest of the ingredients. Pour into a unbaked crust. Bake at 425° for 10 minutes. Lower heat 350°-375° and bake for 30 minutes or until silver knife comes clean after dipping in the pie. Makes one 9-inch pie. Cool before serving.

Easy Pecan Pie

⅓ C. melted butter
⅔ C. sugar
3 eggs
1 C. dark corn syrup

1 C. pecans
Salt
Pie shell

Line an unbaked pie shell with waxed paper. Weight down with about a pound of dired beans. Place on a pre-heated dark cookie sheets on bottom shelf of oven. Bake at 325° for 15 minutes. Save the beans for another pie. Place nuts in pastry shell. Put other ingredients in a food processor. Blend a few seconds and pour over the nuts. Bake at 350° for 45-55 minutes.

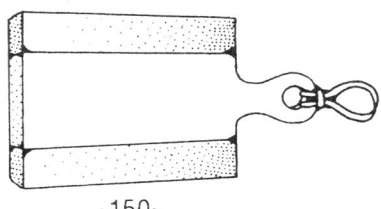

Overnight Brunch

9 slices bread
½ lb. Swiss cheese
½ lb. sharp cheddar cheese
1 lb. bacon (fried and chopped)

6 eggs
3 C. milk
½ tsp. salt

Place bread in 9 x 13-inch pan. Fill up all spaces and corners with extra bread. Lay on cheese and meat. Can use ½ lb. cheese altogether. Mix beaten eggs, milk and salt. Pour over bread and cheese and cover with foil. Put in refrigerator overnight. Bake at 350° for 50 minutes.

Tang Pie

1 graham cracker pie crust
8 oz. sour cream (1 pt.)

1 can Eagle Brand milk
⅓ C. Tang

Mix well and pour into crust; refrigerate.

Rhubarb Pie

3 C. rhubarb
2 C. sugar
2 eggs
2 T. lemon juice
2 T. butter

3 slices bread (broken in pieces)
2-crust pie shell
Milk
Sugar

Mix rhubarb, 2 C. sugar, eggs, lemon juice, butter and bread together and place in unbaked pie shell. Cover with top crust. Glaze with milk and sprinkle with sugar. Bake at 350° for 1 hour.

Depression Cocoa Pudding
(No milk, No eggs)

1 C. sugar
4 T. flour (rounded)
4 T. cocoa (level)
½ tsp. salt

2½ C. boiling water
Margarine (size of walnut)
2 tsp. vanilla

Mix flour, cocoa, sugar and salt; add boiling water slowly and stir well. Cook until thick. Add vanilla and margarine.

Pecan Tarts

DOUGH:
1 stick oleo (less 1-inch to be used
  for filling)

3 oz. cream cheese
1 C. flour

FILLING:
¼ C. sugar
1 inch oleo (1 T.)

1 tsp. vanilla
¾ C. chopped nuts

Mix cream cheese, 1 stick oleo, less 1-inch and flour. Make 24 balls. Place each ball in a muffin mold (tart-pan size) which has been sprayed with non-stick coating. Mix filling ingredients together. Fill dough and bake at 350° for 30 minutes.

Pecan Pie

3 eggs
1 C. light corn syrup
½ C. sugar
1 T. margarine (melted)

1 tsp. vanilla
1⅓ C. pecan halves
Pie shell

Beat eggs lightly. Add syrup, sugar, margarine, vanilla and pecans. Pour into 9-inch unbaked pie shell. Bake at 375° for 40-50 minutes.

Pecan Pie

2 eggs (beaten)
1/8 tsp. salt
½ C. sugar
1 C. pecans

1 C. dark syrup
1 tsp. vanilla
2 T. butter

Combine ingredients and bake in unbaked pie shell in 400° oven for 15 minutes, then 30-35 minutes at 350°.

Crazy Crust

1 C. flour
2 T. sugar
1 tsp. baking powder
½ tsp. salt

¾ C. water
⅔ C. melted margarine
1 egg

Beat together on low for 2 minutes, then on medium until well mixed. Pour batter in pie platter. Carefully spoon in filling. Bake at 350° for 40-45 minutes.

Pecan Pie

¼ C. magarine
¾ C. sugar
1 tsp. vanilla
2 T. flour
3 eggs

½ C Kahlua
½ C. dark corn syrup
¾ C. evaporated milk
1 C. pecans
Pie shell

Cream margarine, sugar, vanilla and flour. Add eggs (1 at a time). Stir in remaining ingredients. Pour into unbaked pie shell. Bake at 400° for 10 minutes. Turn oven down to 325° and bake for 40 minutes more or until set. Makes 1 deep dish pie.

Great Pie Crust

3 C. flour
1¼ C. shortening
¼ tsp. salt

1 tsp. vinegar
1 egg
6 T. water

Blend flour, salt and shortening until about the size of peas. Add remaining ingredients and mix well. Add more water, if necessary, a teaspoon at a time. Divide in half and roll out to desired thickness. Makes two 9-inch crusts.

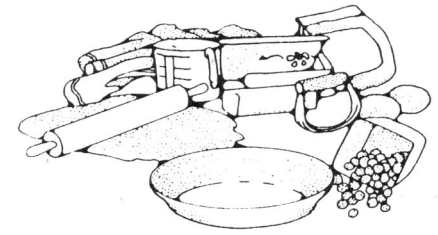

Pie Crust

3 C. flour
1 tsp. salt
1 C. lard

1 egg (slightly beaten)
½ tsp. vinegar
5 T. ice water

Cut lard into flour and salt until particles are the size of peas. Mix in the egg, vinegar and ice water. Gather pastry into a bowl and roll out on floured pastry sheet. Makes 2 double crust pies.

Apple Pie

1 egg
¾ C. sugar
1 tsp. vanilla

½-¾ C. flour
2 tsp. baking powder
1 C. chopped apples and nuts

Beat egg and sugar, add vanilla, flour and baking powder. Mix together and add chopped apples and nuts. Put in greased round cake pan. Bake 25 minutes at 350°.

Strawberry Dream Freeze

1 C. margarine
½ C. brown sugar

2 C. flour
1 C. finely chopped nuts

Beat together for 20 minutes.

2 egg whites

1 tsp. lemon juice

10 oz. pkg. frozen strawberries
1 tsp. vanilla

1 C. sugar
8 oz. carton Cool Whip

Mix first 4 ingredients together. Place in 9 × 13-inch pan. Bake at 400° for 15 minutes. Stir crumbs about while baking. When brown remove from oven. Place ½ mixture loosely in bottom of pan. Whip together for 20 minutes, the egg white, lemon juice, strawberries, sugar and vanilla. When whipped fold in one small carton of Cool Whip. Pour over crumb mixture. Top with remaining crumbs. Cover well and freeze. Place in ice box 1 hour before serving.

Easy Brunch

4 slices bacon (sliced)
½ lb. chipped beef (coarsely sliced)
¼ C. butter
1 lb. fresh mushrooms (sliced and
   sauteed)
½ C. flour

1 qt. whole milk
16 eggs
1 C. evaporated milk
¼ tsp. salt
¼ C. melted butter
Pepper

Saute bacon and drain; remove from pan. In the same pan add chipped beef, butter and ¾ of the mushrooms. Sprinkle flour and pepper over mixture. Gradually stir in whole milk. Heat mixture, stirring until thick and smooth. Set aside. Combine eggs with salt and evaporated milk and scramble in butter. In a 3-qt. casserole dish, alternate layers of eggs and sauce, ending with sauce. Garnish with reserved mushrooms. Refrigerate overnight. Before serving, cover and bake 1-1½ hours at 275°.

Crunchee Egg Brunch

2 C. frozen hash browns (thawed)
6 hard cooked eggs (whites and yolks separated, whites thinly sliced, mash yolks with fork)
1 (8 oz.) can water chestnuts (thinly sliced)
1 can cream of onion soup (undiluted)
¼ C. sour cream
¼ C. melted butter

1 T. creamy horseradish suace
¼ C. green pepper (diced)
¼ C. green onion (chopped)
2 T. butter
6 slices bacon (fried and crumbled)
Pepper to taste
½ C. shredded cheddar cheese
½ C. crushed rice cereal

Place hash browns on the bottom of a 2½-qt. casserole. Top with thinly sliced egg whites and water chestnuts. Combine the cream of onion soup, sour cream, horseradish sauce and egg yolks. Saute green pepper and onion in butter. Add to soup mixture; mix well. Pour over mixture in casserole. Sprinkle crumbled bacon on top and add pepper to taste. Combine shredded cheese and rice cereal together and place on top of bacon. Drizzle melted butter over cereal. Bake at 375° for 30 minutes or until bubbly and brown. Garnish with parsley. Serves 4-6.

Rice Chex Dessert

TOPPING AND CRUST:
2½ C. crushed Rice Chex cereal
1 stick margarine
1 C. coconut

¾ C. brown sugar
½ C. chopped nuts

FILLING:
1 C. powdered sugar
8 oz. cream cheese

12 oz. whipped topping
1 can cherry pie filling

Mix crust ingredients until crumbly. Pat into 9 x 13-inch pan reserving 1 C. for topping. Mix powdered sugar, cream cheese and whipped topping until smooth and put on the ceereal crust. Cover with the cherry pie filling and top with the remaining crumbs.

BARS, COOKIES, 'N CANDY

Bars, Cookies, 'N Candy

Bars, Cookies, 'N Candy - Continued

"Just For Notes"

Pumpkin Cookies

1 C. shortening
2 C. sugar
2 C. cooked pumpkin
2 tsp. vanilla
4 C. flour

2 tsp. baking soda
2 tsp. cinnamon
1 (12 oz.) pkg. chocolate chips
   and nuts (opt.)

Cream shortening and sugar. Stir in pumpkin and vanilla. Sift flour, soda and cinnamon. Stir into mixture. Add chocolate chips and nuts. Drop by spoonfuls onto greased cookie sheet. Bake at 375° for 12-15 minutes. Makes 48 cookies.

Chocolate Drop Cookies

1 C. brown sugar
1 egg
½ tsp. baking soda
1½ C. flour
½ C. chopped nutmeats

½ C. butter or margarine
3 tsp. cocoa
1 tsp. baking powder
½ C. sour cream
½ tsp. vanilla

Combine all ingredients and drop by teaspoonful on a greased baking sheet. Bake in a 350° oven for 10 minutes. Makes 3½ dozen. (NOTE: May be frosted with a chocolate cream icing, if desired.)

Crispy Easter Nests

1 (7 oz.) jar marshmallow creme
¼ C. creamy peanut butter
2 T. margarine (melted)

1 (5 oz.) can chow mein noodles
1 C. plain holiday pastel M & M candies
Peanut pastel M & M canies

Combine marshmallow creme, peanut butter and margarine. Mix until well blended. Add noodles and 1 C. plain pastel M & M candies. Mix well. Drop by ⅓ cupfuls onto greased cookie sheet. Shape with buttered fingers to form nests. Fill with peanut pastel M & M candies before serving. Makes 10-12 nests.

Fudge Nut Mounds

⅔ C. margarine
1 C. cottage cheese
2 tsp. vanilla
2¾ C. flour
½ tsp. salt
½ C. chopped nuts

1⅔ C. granulated sugar
2 eggs
½ C. cocoa
1 tsp. baking powder
½ C. chocolate chips
Powdered sugar

Mix at medium speed, butter, sugars. Beat in cottage cheese, then eggs, vanilla. Sift flour, cocoa, baking powder, salt. beat into butter mixture at low speed. Add chocolate bits and nuts. Divide dough, for ease of handling, into several parts. Wrap in waxed paper or foil and refrigerate until firm. Set oven to 350°. Roll dough into 1¼-inch balls. Roll ball in powdered sugar, covering them with a thick coating. Place on greased cookie sheet. Bake for 15 minutes.

Molasses Cookies

1 C. lard	2 tsp. soda
1 C. sugar	½ tsp. ginger
1 egg	½ tsp. cloves
½ C. hot water	5½ C. flour (about)

Cream lard and sugar. Add egg, molasses and water and blend well. Stir flour, soda, ginger and cloves and add to the above. Refrigerate for 1 hour or overnight. Roll out on floured board to about ¼-inch thick and cut with favorite cookie cutter. Bake at 400° for about 10 minutes. May be frosted or stored in tightly covered container.

Reese's Peanut Butter Chip Chocolate Cookies

1 C. butter/margarine	⅔ C. Hershey's cocoa
1½ C. sugar	¾ tsp. baking soda
2 eggs	½ tsp. salt
2 tsp. vanilla	2 C. (12 oz. pkg.) peanut butter
2 C. unsifted all-purpose flour	chips

Cream butter or margarine, sugar, eggs and vanilla until light and fluffy Combine flour, cocoa, baking soda and salt; add to creamed mixture. Stir in peanut butter chips. Chill until firm enough to handle. Shape small amounts of dough into 1-inch balls. Place on ungreased baking sheet and flatten slightly with fork. Bake at 350° for 8-10 minutes. Cool 1 minute before removing from cookie sheet onto wire rack. Makes about 6 dozen 2½-inch cookies.

Peanut Butter Cookies

1½ C. sifted all-purpose flour
1½ tsp. baking powder
½ tsp. salt
¼ C. margarine
½ C. creamy peanut butter

½ tsp. grated, fresh orange
1½ tsp. pure vanilla
1 egg (well beaten)
⅓ C. orange juice
Artificial sweetener to substitute
  for 24 tsp. sugar

Preheat oven to 400°. Sift together flour, baking powder and salt. Cream together margarine, peanut butter, orange rind and vanilla. Add egg, orange juice and artificial sweetener; blend well. Add dry ingredients gradually; mix well after each addition. Measure 1 T. (level) dough for each cookie. Roll between hands to form ball. Place 2-inches apart on ungreased cookie sheet; flatten with fork. Bake about 15 minutes. Store cookies in a tightly covered tin. These cookies have better flavor and texture 24 hours after baking. Yield: 24 cookies.

Sugar Cookies

CREAM TOGETHER:
1 C. sugar
1 C. butter
Add 2 eggs

1 C. powdered sugar
1 C. oil

SIFT TOGETHER:
4½ C. flour
1 tsp. cream of tartar

1 tsp. baking soda
1 tsp. vanilla (last)

Refrigerate overnight. Roll in balls and roll in sugar and press with a fork. Bake.

Peanut Butter Chocolate Chip Cookies

1¼ C. flour
¾ tsp. baking soda
½ tsp. baking powder
¼ tsp. salt
¾ C. peanut butter
½ C. butter (softened; can use
  Crisco butter)

½ C. sugar
½ C. brown sugar
½ tsp. vanilla
5 T. milk
1 egg
1 C. chocolate chips
½ C. chopped nuts

Combine flour, baking soda and powder in large bowl. Cream together peanut butter, butter, sugar, brown sugar in large bowl. Beat in milk, egg and vanilla. Add flour mixture. Then add chips and nuts. Bake at 350° for 10-12 minutes or until golden brown.

Big Cookie

1 T. peanut butter
2 T. + 2 tsp. non-fat dry milk
2 T. raisins
½ tsp. baking powder
2 T. water

2 tsp. brown sugar or honey or
  sugar substitute
¾ oz. oatmeal (uncooked,
  old fashioned)

Preheat oven to 350°. In medium bowl combine all ingredients. Spray cookie sheet with Pam, drop mixture on sheet. Bake 10 minutes. Equals one serving, 1 protein, 1 bread, 1 fat, ½ milk, 1 fruit, optional calories 40 (brown sugar or honey).

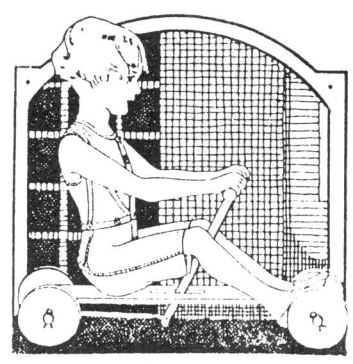

Unbaked Caramel Cookies

2 C. sugar
¾ C. oleo
⅔ C. evaporated milk

4 oz. pkg. instant pudding
(butterscotch or chocolate)
3½ C. raw oatmeal

In large saucepan combine sugar, oleo, milk. Bring to boil for 5 minutes. Remove from heat, add pudding mix and oatmeal. Cool slightly. Drop by teaspoon on waxed paper. Let set until firm. Store in refrigerator. 1 C. coconut may also be added or nuts.

No Bake Corn Flake Cookies

½ C. white Karo
½ C. white sugar
2 T. cocoa

½ C. peanut butter
3 C. corn flakes

Place Karo, sugar and cocoa in saucepan and bring to a boil. Then remove from heat. Stir in peanut butter and corn flakes. Drop on waxed paper to cool.

No Bake Cookies

2 C. white sugar
½ C. milk

¼-½ C. cocoa
¼ C. butter

Cook for 2 minutes. then remove from heat and add:

½ C. chunky peanut butter
3 C. oatmeal

1 tsp. vanilla

Drop by spoonfuls on waxed paper to cool. Makes 2 dozen.

Orange Slice Cookies

1½ C. brown sugar
½ C. shortening
2 eggs
2 C. flour
1 tsp. soda

½ tsp. salt
1 lb. orange slice candy
½ C. flaked coconut or nuts
½ C. quick oatmeal

Cream sugar and shortening. Beat in eggs. Sift 1½ C. flour, soda and salt. Blend into creamed mixture. Cut orange slices into small pieces and mix with remaining ½ C. flour. Add with remaining ingredients. Drop by teaspoon onto greased cookie sheet. Bake at 325° for 10-12 minutes. Yields: 5 dozen.

Honey Cookies

1 C. honey
3¾ C. flour
4¾ tsp. baking powder
¼ tsp. baking soda

1 C. shortening (Crisco or lard)
½ tsp. each: cinnamon, cloves,
  and allspice

Heat honey and shortening together about 1 minute. Cool. Sift flour, baking powder and soda; also spices together. Add to first mixture to make a soft dough. Roll thin, cut and bake at 350° for 12-15 minutes. Yield; 6 dozen cookies. Frost with powdered sugar frosting.

Old Fashioned Oatmeal Cookies

1 C. raisins	1 tsp. soda
1 C. water	1 tsp. salt
¾ C. shortening	1 tsp. cinnamon
1½ C. sugar	½ tsp. baking powder
2 eggs	½ tsp. cloves
1 tsp. vanilla	2 C. oats
2½ C. flour	½ C. chopped nuts

Simmer raisins and water over medium heat until raisins are plump about 15 minutes. Drain raisins, reserving the liquid. Add enough water if needed to measure ½ C. Heat oven to 400°. Mix thoroughly shortening, sugar, eggs and vanilla. Stir in reserved liquid. Blend in remaining ingredients. Drop dough by rounded teaspoonful about 2-inches apart onto greased baking sheets. Bake 8-10 minutes or until brown. About 6½ dozen cookies.

Candy Cane Cookies

Preheat oven to 375°. Mix together thoroughly:

1 C. shortening (half butter)	1 tsp. vanilla
1 C. sifted confectioner's sugar	1½ tsp. almond extract
1 egg	

Sift together and stir in 2½ C. sifted flour, 1 tsp. salt. Divide dough in two halves. Blend into one half ½ tsp. red food coloring. Roll 1 tsp. each color dough into a strip about 4-inches long. Place strips side by side; press together and twist like a rope. Place on ungreased cookie sheet. Curve top down to form cane handle. Bake 9 minutes until down. Roll in mixture of ½ C. sugar, ½ C. crushed peppermint candy.

Christmas Butter Cookies

1¾ C. flour
½ tsp. baking powder
⅔ C. butter

½ C. sugar
1 small egg (well beaten)
½ tsp. vanilla

Sift flour with baking powder. Cream butter well; add sugar and continue creaming until well mixed. Mix in the beaten egg. Add vanilla. Stir in sifted dry ingredients in 2 or 3 portions until dough is just smooth. Roll out to 1/8-inch thick on a floured surface and cut into desired shapes. Bake on ungreased cookie sheet in a moderately hot oven (400°) for 6-8 minutes or until delicately browned. Makes 3-4 dozen cookies.

Cake Mix Cookies

1 large box cake mix
2 eggs
½ tsp. soda

½ C. margarine (melted)
½ C. flour

Beat all ingredients together. Roll in ball. Place about 1-inch apart on ungreased cookie sheet. Bake at 350° for 10 minutes.

Oatmeal Crispies

1 C. shortening
1 C. brown sugar
1 C. white sugar
2 eggs (well beaten)
1½ C. flour

1 tsp. vanilla
1 tsp. salt
1 tsp. soda
3 C. quick oatmeal
½ C. nuts

Mix in order. Bake at 350° for 10 minutes.

Ginger Cookies

2½ C. flour
½ tsp. salt
1 tsp. cinnamon
1 C. brown sugar
¼ C. molasses
¼ C. sugar

2 tsp. soda (baking)
3 tsp. ginger
¾ C. butter
1 egg
1 T. lemon rind or 2 tsp. lemon
    juice

Perheat oven to 350°. Mix flour, soda, salt, ginger and cinnamon in bowl. Cream butter, brown sugar and egg in another bowl until fluffy. Beat in molasses and lemon rind. Stir in dry ingredients, half at a time; blend well after each time. Roll level teaspoonfuls of dough between palms into balls; roll in sugar. Place on ungreased cookie sheet. Bake for 10 minutes.

Rhubarb Cookies

½ C. shortening
1 C. brown sugar
1 egg
½ tsp. salt
½ tsp. cinnamon
¼ tsp. cloves
½ tsp. nutmeg

2 C. flour
1 tsp. baking soda
¼ C. milk
1 C. chopped nuts
1 C. raisins
1 C. finely chopped rhubarb
¼ C. flaked coconut

Cream shortening and sugar. Add egg and mix well. Sift together dry ingredients and add alternately with milk. Fold in nuts, raisins, rhubarb and coconut. Drop by teaspoons on greased cookie sheets. Bake at 375° for 10-12 minutes. Makes 4½ dozen.

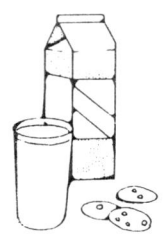

Oatmeal Cookies

2 C. brown sugar
2 C. oatmeal
2 C. flour
½ C. shortening
½ C. margarine

2 eggs (beaten)
1 tsp. soda
2 T. hot water
1 C. ground dates
½ C. nuts.

Mix shortening and margarine together. Mix sugar, oatmeal, flour and shortening, cutting until pea size. Dissolve soda in hot water; add eggs. Mix and add to first mixture. Add dates and nuts. You may refrigerate dough. Pat dough out and cut. Bake at 375° for 5-10 minutes.

Shake Ups

1 C. sugar
1 C. brown sugar
1 C. oleo
2 eggs
2 tsp. vanilla

2 C. rolled oats
2 C. flour
2 C. corn flakes
2 tsp. soda
½ tsp. salt

Cream together the sugars, oleo, eggs and vanilla. Shake tgether all the dry ingredients in brown bag. (Raisins, coconut, chocolate chips and nuts may be added to dry ingredients.) Add dry mixture to creamed mixture. Drop by teaspoonful on a greased baking sheet and bake in a 350° oven for 10 minutes.

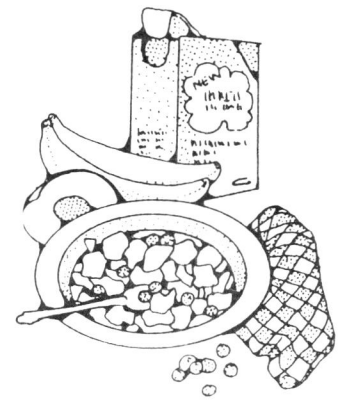

Cake Mixture Cookies

Cake mix   1 tsp. vanilla
⅓ C. oil   2 eggs

Combine ½ of cake mix with other ingredients. Mix well. Add rest of mix. If you wish, add nut meats, raisins, chocolate bits or butterscotch bits. Drop by teaspoon on slightly greased cookie sheet. Bake in preheated 350° oven for 8 minutes for chewy; 10 minutes for crisp.

Oatmeal Cookies

1 C. white sugar   1 tsp. vanilla
1 C. brown sugar   2 C. flour
¾ C. margarine   1 tsp. baking soda
½ C. crunchy peanut butter   1 tsp. cinnamon
2 eggs   1 tsp. salt
¼ C. milk   1½ C. oats
                                    1 C. raisins

Cream margarine, sugars and peanut butter. Add eggs, one at a time. Beat in milk and vanilla. Mix flour, salt, soda and cinnamon. Stir in oats and raisins. Drop by heaping tablespoons on a greased cookie sheet, 2-inches apart. Bake at 350° for 15 minutes. Makes 40 cookies.

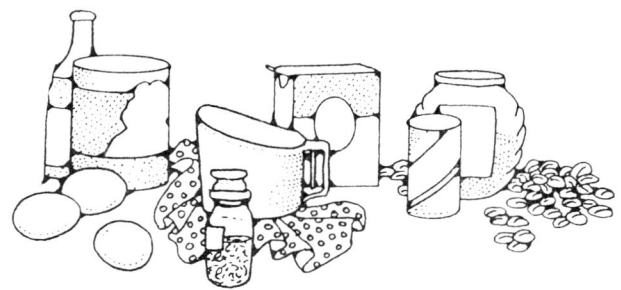

Oatmeal Crispies Ice Box Cookies

1 C. shortening
1 C. brown sugar
1 C. white sugar
2 beaten eggs
1 tsp. vanilla

1½ C. flour
1 tsp. salt
1 tsp. soda
3 C. quick oatmeal
½ C. chopped nuts

Cream sugars and shortening. Add eggs and vanilla and beat well. Add dry ingredients and nuts. Shape in 2 rolls, wrap in waxed paper and chill overnight. Slice thin and bake at 350° about 10 minutes.

Sugar Cookies

1 C. oleo
1 C. Crisco
1 C. white sugar
1 C. powdered sugar

2 eggs
2 tsp. vanilla
4 C. flour
1 tsp. soda
1 tsp. cream of tartar

Cream oleo, Crisco, white sugar and powdered sugar (I usually sift mine). Add eggs and vanilla. Mix well. Pour in flour, soda and cream of tartar; mix well. Make into small balls. Place on greased cookie sheets. Flatten with glass dipped in sugar. Red and green sugar is nice for Christmas. Bake at 350° until edges turn golden brown (approximately 10-12 minutes.)

Sugar Cookies

1 C. oleo (not butter or shortening)   *1 egg*
2 C. powdered sugar   *2½ C. sifted flour*
½ tsp. soda   *1 tsp. vanilla*

Cream oleo, powdered sugar and soda together until smooth. Add egg and beat until smooth. Mix in vanilla. Add flour and stir until smooth. Form into balls and smash with a glass dipped in sugar on an ungreased baking sheet or refrigerate 1 hour or more. Roll and cut with cookie cutters. Decorate with colored sugars if desired or frost after baking. Bake 8-10 minutes in a 350° oven. Watch closely as they brown easily.

Chocolate Brownies

¾ C. cocoa   *2 eggs*
½ tsp. soda   *1⅓ C. flour*
⅔ C. margarine (melted)   *½ tsp. salt*
½ C. boiling water   *1 tsp. vanilla*
1½ C. sugar

Mix cocoa and soda. Blend in ⅓ C. margarine. Add ½ C. boiling water. Stir this until it thickens. Stir in sugar, eggs and remaining ⅓ C. margarine. Stir until smooth. Add flour, vanilla and salt. Bake at 350° in a 9 × 13 × 2-inch pan for 20-25 minutes.

Coconut Candy

1 stick butter   *2 squares semi-sweet chocolate*
2 C. powdered sugar   *(melted)*
8 oz. coconut

Melt butter in saucepan. Remove from heat. Add sugar and coconut. Mix well. Shape teaspoonful into balls. Make indent in center and place on cookie sheet. Fill centers with melted chocolate. Chill until firm. Store in refrigerator. Makes 3 dozen.

Joyce's Bars

1 stick butter or margarine	*6 oz. pkg. butterscotch chips*
1 C. crushed graham crackers	*1 can sweetened condensed milk*
1 C. coconut	*1 C. chopped nuts or pecans*
6 oz. pkg. chocolate chips	

Using an 8 × 11-inch pan, place 1 stick of butter in it and melt in oven. Sprinkle crushed graham crackers over the melted butter. Next sprinkle the coconut and then the chips. On top of these drizzle sweetened condensed milk. Cover with chopped nuts and bake for 30-35 minutes at 350°. Cool in the pan before attempting to cut into bars or squares.

No Bake Fudge Cookies

2 C. sugar	*1 tsp. vanilla*
1 C. milk	*1 C. nutmeats*
2 squares unsweetened chocolate	*24 marshmallows (cut up)*
1/8 tsp. salt	*3 C. graham cracker crumbs*
1 T. butter	

Combine sugar, milk, chocolate and salt and boil to soft ball stage. Add butter and vanilla. Pour mixture over marshmallows, nuts and crumbs. Mix well. Drop by spoonfuls on waxed paper. Cool.

Brunch Bars

2 eggs	½ tsp. salt
1½ C. sugar	1 tsp. vanilla
2¼ C. flour	Can of fruit cocktail
½ tsp. soda	

TOPPING:
1½ C. coconut   ½ C. chopped nuts

GLAZE:
1½ C. sugar   2 sticks margarine
½ C. evaporated milk

For Bars: Beat eggs until light and fluffy. Blend can of fruit cocktail in blender 5-10 seconds. Then beat whole mixture together. Put in 11 x 15-inch cookie sheet pan lightly greased and floured. Top with coconut and nuts. Bake 30-35 minutes in 350° oven. Cool bar and top with glaze.

For Glaze: Boil ingredients in glaze 2 minutes, cool and spread on top of bars.

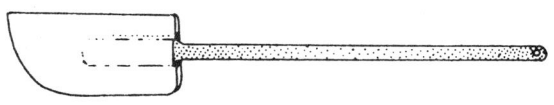

Yummy Bars

¾ C. white sugar	¼ tsp. salt
½ C. shortening	2 T. cocoa
2 eggs	½ C. coconut
1 tsp. vanilla	½ C. nuts (opt.)

TOPPING:
1 jar marshmallow creme   1 C. peanut butter
1 C. chocolate chips   1½ C. Rice Krispies
1 C. butterscotch chips

Cream together sugar, shortening, eggs and vanilla. Add remaining ingredients and beat well. Bake in a 9 x 13-inch cake pan 15-20 minutes at 350°. When cool, spread with marshmallow creme. Melt remaining ingredients together in double boiler. Add slightly crumbled Rice Krispies. Spread over bars and refrigerate.

Jiffy Chewy Bars

1 pkg. Jiffy yellow cake mix	¼ C. brown sugar
1 T. water	1 T. oleo
2 T. flour	1 T. corn syrup
¼ C. chocolate chips	¼-½ C. nuts
1 egg	

Mix all together. Bake in 8×8-inch pan at 350° for 25-30 minutes.

Vera's Cookies

1 stick oleo	1 C. nuts
1 C. graham crackers	1 C. chocolate chips
1 C. coconut	1 can Eagle Brand milk

Melt oleo in 9×13-inch pan. Sprinkle graham crackers over oleo, add coconut, nuts, chocolate bits and drizzle milk over top of mixture. Bake at 350° for 30 minutes. Cut while warm.

Rhubarb Bars

1 C. flour	2 eggs (beaten)
½ C. margarine	1½ C. sugar
5 T. powdered sugar	¼ C. flour
1/8 tsp. salt	3 C. diced rhubarb

Blend flour, margarine, powdered sugar and salt. Put in 12×8-inch pan. Bake 10 minutes at 375°. Remove from oven and spread over the crust the filling made by beating the eggs and add the other ingredients. Stir in rhubarb last. Bake at 350°, about 30 minutes. Gets sugary crust on top.

Pat's Brownies

1 pkg. German chocolate cake mix   *¾ C. melted butter*
⅓ C. evaporated milk   *1 bag walnut pieces*

Mix the above ingredients altogether.

1 (12 oz.) bag semi-sweet chocolate chips

Mix the following together by melting:
1 bag caramels   *⅓ C. evaporated milk*

Press half of first mix into greased floured pan, 9 × 13-inch. Bake at 350° for 7 minutes. Sprinkle chocolate chips over top. Pour the melted caramels and milk mixture over the chocolate chips. Take the other half of top mixture and crumble over top of caramel. Bake for 7 minutes more. Don't overbake or they will get hard.

Raisin Bars

Cook until thick:
1 C. sugar   *3 T. flour*
2 C. raisins   *1 C. water*

Let cool while making crust.

Crust:
1 C. brown sugar   *¾ C. melted margarine*
1 tsp. salt. ½ tsp. soda dissolved in
¼ C. oatmeal   *1 tsp. hot water*
1½ C. flour   *1 tsp. vanilla*

Mix crust ingredients well, spread ½ of mixture in a greased 9 × 13-inch pan. Pour raisin sauce over crust, add rest of crust to top - it will be crumbly Bake 25 minutes or until crust is brown, at 350°.

Devil's Food Bars

1 devil's food cake mix   *¾ C. creamy peanut butter*
1 stick butter or margarine (melted)   *1 (7 or 7½ oz.) jar marshmallow creme*

Combine melted butter and dry cake mix. Reserve 1½ C. of this topping for top crust. Pat remaining crumb mixture into ungreased 9 × 13 × 2-inch pan. Top that layer with combined peanut butter and marshmallow creme and spread evenly. Crumble remaining mixture over that. Bake 20 minutes at 350°. Cool. Makes 3 dozen bars.

Peanut Butter Bars

½ C. butter or margarine
½ C. sugar
½ C. brown sugar
1 egg
⅓ C. peanut butter
½ tsp. soda

½ tsp. salt
½ tsp. vanilla
1 C. flour
1 C. oatmeal
6 oz. pkg. chocolate chips

Cream butter and sugars; add egg and beat well. Add peanut butter and mix well. Combine dry ingredients and add to creamed mixture. Mix well and add vanilla. Pour into greased 9-inch squares pan. Bake at 350° for 20-25 minutes. Sprinkle with chocolate chips. Let stand 5 minutes, then spread evenly. Frost bars. (Double the recipe and it will make enough for jelly roll pan.)

FROSTING:
½ C. powdered sugar
3-4 T. milk

¼ C. peanut butter

Mix ingredients together until smooth.

Butterscotch Bars

2 eggs
¾ C. margarine
1 C. sugar

2½ C. graham crackers
½ C. coconut
2 C. small marshmallows
½ C. nuts

1 pkg. butterscotch chips

2 T peanut butter

Put eggs, margarine and sugar in saucepan. Boil slowly for 2 minutes. Let cool. After first mixture is cooled and crushed graham crackers, coconut, marshmallows and nuts. Mix all together in bowl. Press this into 9 x 13-inch pan. Melt chips and peanut butter together and spread this over mixture and cool. No Baking!

Bathtime Brownies

Brownie mix
3½ C. powdered sugar
8 T. soft oleo
4-6 T. milk

1 tsp. peppermint flavor
5-6 drops food coloring
12 oz. chocolate chips
6 T. oleo

Mix brownies according to package directions and cool. Mix together the powdered sugar, 8 T. oleo, milk, flavoring and desired coloring to make a smooth thick frosting. Frost cool brownies and place in refrigerator to harden. Melt chocolate chips and remaining oleo together. Mix thoroughly and spread on top of the frosting. Allow to harden.

Betty's Peanut Butter Bars

½ C. butter
½ C. sugar
½ C. brown sugar
½ tsp. soda
1 C. flour

½ tsp. vanilla
1 egg
⅓ C. peanut butter
¼ tsp. salt
1 C. oatmeal

Mix all of the above ingredients and press mixture into 9 x 13-inch pan. Bake at 350° for 15-20 minutes. Take out when they begin to puff up and turn faintly brown. Pour 1 pkg. chocolate chips over bars while they are hot. Spread chocolate when it melts. Mix together ½ C. powdered sugar, ½ C. peanut butter, 4-6 T. milk. Dribble over top of bars.

Oh Henry Bars

4 C. quick oatmeal
½ tsp. salt
½ C. white Karo syrup

⅔ C. oleo (melted)
1 C. brown sugar

TOPPING:
1 (12 oz.) pkg. chocolate chips

¾ C. peanut butter

Mix ingredients and pour in greased 9 × 13-inch glass pan. Bake at 425° for 10 minutes. Cool. Melt chocolate chips and peanut butter. Pour on to and let set.

Brownies

1½ C. sifted flour
8 T. cocoa
1 tsp. salt
2 C. sugar

1 C. softened margarine
4 unbeaten eggs
2 tsp. vanilla
1 C. nuts (opt.)

Preheat oven to 325°. Grease or spray with cooking spray, the bottom and sides of an oblong glsss baking dish. Combine dry ingredients. Combine margarine, eggs and sugar. Mix. Add dry ingredients, vanilla and nuts. Mix. Batter will be thick. Pour into baking dish spreadeing evenly. Bake 30-35 minutes. Do Not Overbake. Frost with your favorite frosting or sprinkle with powdered sugar.

Iced Apple Brownies

3 eggs
1¾ C. sugar
1 C. oil
1 tsp. cinnamon
1 C. chopped nuts

2 C. flour
1 tsp. salt
1 tsp. baking soda
1 C. finely chopped apples

Cream eggs with sugar and oil. Add cinnamon and nuts. Stir in dry ingredients and apples. Pour into a 9×13-inch pan (greased) and bake in 350° preheated oven for 35-40 minutes.

ICING:
¼ C. butter
1 (3 oz.) pkg. cream cheese
  (softened)

1 C. nuts (finely chopped)
½ box (8 oz.) powdered sugar
1 tsp. vanilla

Beat all ingredients with mixer until smooth. Spread on cooled brownies.

Graham Crax Bars

½ C. butter
1 C. brown sugar
1 C. crushed graham crackers

⅓ C. milk
1 C. flaked coconut

Cook 5 minutes, stir all the time. Spread between layers of graham crackers. Top with powdered sugar and cocoa frosting. Cut into bars.

Creamy Chocolate Mint Melts

1½ lbs. almond bark
1 C. chocolate chips (6 oz. pkg.)
1 tsp. peppermint extract

4 drops green food coloring
3 T. whipping cream or milk

Line bottom and sides of 12 × 8-inch glass dish with waxed paper. Combine ⅔ of almond bark and the chocolate chips, melt and stir until smooth. Spread ½ in bottom of lined baking dish, refrigerate to set, about 20 minutes. Soften remaining almond bark, stir in extract and coloring. Add cream or milk until spreading consistency. Spread over chocolate. Refrigerate until set, about 20 minutes. Spread rest of chocolate mixture over mint. Chill until set. Bring to room temperature before cutting.

Lemon Crumb Squares

1 can sweetened milk
½ C. lemon juice
1 tsp. lemon peel
1½ C. flour
1 tsp. baking powder

½ tsp. salt
⅔ C. butter
1 C. brown sugar
1 C. uncooked oatmeal

Blend together condensed milk, juice and lemon peel. Set aside. Cream butter, add sugar and blend well. Add oatmeal. Sift flour, baking powder and salt. Add to oatmeal mixture. Mix until crumbly. Put in pan. Spread. Save some of crumb mixture. Spread lemon mixture on top. Cover with rest of crumb mixture. Bake at 350° for 25 minutes until brown around edges. Cool in pan for 15 minutes. Cut into squares and chill in pan until firm.

Frosted Strawberry Squares

2 (3 oz. ea.) pkgs. strawberry
    gelatin
1 (3 oz.) pkg. lemon gelatin
2 (10 oz. ea.) pkgs. frozen
    strawberries
1 (3 oz.) pkg. cream cheese

3 C. boiling water
1 C. boiling water
1 (8 oz.) can crushed pineapple
1 container whipped cream

Dissolve strawberry gelatin in 3 C. boiling water. Immediately add frozen strawberries, stirring until completely thawed. Pour into lightly oiled 13 x 9-inch pan. Chill until partially set. Meanwhile, drain pineapple, reserving juice. Dissolve lemon gelatin in 1 C. boiling water. Stir in pineapple. Chill until thick and syrupy. Fold in whipped cream. Spread over gelatin in pan and chill until set. Makes 12 servings.

Butterscotch Squares

1 (12 oz.) pkg. butterscotch chips
⅓ C. margarine
2 C. graham cracker crumbs
1 C. chopped nuts

1 (8 oz.) pkg. cream cheese
1 (14 oz.) can Eagle brand milk
1 tsp. vanilla
1 egg

Preheat oven to 350°. Melt chips and margarine. Stir in cracker crumbs and nuts. Press ½ of mixture into 9 x 13-inch pan (greased). In large bowl, beat cheese until fluffy. Beat in milk, vanilla and egg. Mix well, pour into prepared pan. Cover with rest of crumb mixture. Bake 25-30 minutes or until toothpick comes out clean. Cool to room temperature. Chill before cutting.

Chocolate Cherry Creams

1 (6 oz.) pkg. semi-sweet chocolate
   morsels
½ C. evaporated milk
2½ C. powdered sugar (sifted)

⅓ C. nuts (chopped)
⅓ C. maraschino cherries (cut up)
1¼ C. coconut (cut up)

Put semi-sweet chocolate morsels and evaporated milk into a heavy 2-qt. saucepan. Stir over low heat until chocolate melts completely. Remove from heat. Stir in sifted powdered sugar (mix well), chopped nuts and well drained cut up maraschino cherries. Chill until mixture is firm enough to handle (about 1 hour). Roll teaspoonfuls of mixture into a the cut up coconut. Chill until firm, about 4 hours. Makes 30.

Bon Bon's

2 sticks oleo
2 boxes (1 lb.) powdered sugar
1 can Eagle Brand condensed milk

1 tsp. vanilla
1 pkg. coconut
1 C. nuts

DIP:
2 (6 oz. ea.) pkg. chocolate chips

1 slab paraffin

Melt oleo; add powdered sugar, condensed milk, vanilla, coconut and nuts. Chill for several hours or overnight. Roll into balls about the size of small walnuts and place on wax paper linged cookie sheets. Put back in refrigerator until you are ready to dip them. While you are making the balls, melt the chocolate chips and paraffin over hot water and keep it hot while you are dipping. Stick a sharp pointed instrument (nut pick, toothpick, etc.) into bottom of candy (or the top) and dip quickly itno the chocolate dip. Roll slightly to cover nicely and place back on wax paper. These store or freeze nicely.

Carolyn's Caramel Corn

2 C. brown sugar
½ C. white syrup
2 sticks oleo

1/8 cream of tartar
1 tsp. soda
5 qt. popped corn

Combine sugar, syrup, oleo and cream of tartar. Boil rapidly for 5 minutes; remove from heat. Add the soda and stir well. Will foam up and get lighter in color. Pour over popped corn. Mix well and bake at 250° for 1 hour, stirring every 15 minutes.

Karen's Goodies

1 stick oleo
6 oz. pkg. chocolate chips
2 C. powdered sugar

½ C. peanut butter
6 C. Rice Chex

Melt oleo, chocolate chips and peanut butter in double boiler or microwave. Pour melted mixture over Rice Chex and mix until Rice Chex is coated but not crushed. Drop into a paper bag and pour powdered sugar over all. Shake the bag gently until cereal is coated. Let cool and enjoy.

White Fudge

2 C. sugar
1 C. evaporated milk
½ C. butter or margarine
8 oz. almond bark

1 C. miniature marshmallows
½ C. flaked coconut
½ C. chopped nuts
1 tsp. vanilla

Cook sugar, milk and butter to 234° or softball stage. Add remainder of ingredients and stir until bark and marshmallows are melted. Pour into buttered or oiled 8×12-inch or 9×12-inch pan or baking dish. Let harden and cut in squares. Flavor improves, if allowed to set in cold places in a tight container or it freezes nicely.

Before Bed Divinity

4 C. sugar
1 C. light corn syrup
¾ C. water

3 egg whites (beaten)
1 tsp. vanilla
½ C. chopped nuts

Combine sugar, light corn syrup and water; cook over low heat. Stir until sugar is dissolved. Cook, without stirring at 225°. Remove from heat and add egg whites, beating constantly. Continue beating until mixture holds its shape and loses its gloss. Add vanilla and nuts. Drop by teaspoonfuls on lightly buttered pan.

Divinity Candy

4 C. sugar
1 C. white Karo
1 C. water

1 C. nuts
1 tsp. vanilla
4 egg whites (beaten)

Boil sugar, Karo and water to 310° or until there is a cracking sound when dropped in cold water. Pour slowly into beaten egg whites. Add nuts and vanilla. Continue beating until it holds shape. My mother would not make this candy on a cloudy day. There had to be sunshine and fair weather or it would not set or harden according to her.

Peanut Butter Fudge

1 C. white sugar
1 C. brown sugar
Pinch of salt
½ C. peanut butter

2 T. butter
1 T. vanilla
1 C. marshmallows
¼ C. evaporated milk

Cook sugar, butter and milk to a soft ball - 240°. Add salt, vanilla and mix. Add marshmallows and peanut butter. Remove from heat and beat until thick. Pour into pan and let stand until hard.

Anise Candy

3 C. sugar	*1 tsp. red coloring*
1 C. white syrup	*1 tsp. anise extract or a few drops*
½ C. water	*anise oil*

Boil to hard crack. Add red coloring and anise oil fast. Do not stir. Pour in an ungreased pan or cookie sheet. Let harden and break into pieces. Be sure candy has reached the hard crack stage or it will not be brittle enough. When candy is done it will crack when you test it in cold water.

Nut Caramels

¼ C. oleo	*¼ tsp. salt*
1 C. evaporated milk	*¼ tsp. vanilla*
1 C. sugar	*1 C. pecans*
1 C. dark corn sryup	

Generously butter an 8-inch square pan. In a small saucepan, heat butter and evaporated milk until butter is melted. In separate 2-qt. saucepan cook, sugar, corn syrup and salt over medium heat until it reaches firm ball stage, 244°, stirring often. Slowly stir in milk mixture, so sugar mixture does not stop boiling. Stirring constantly, cook mixture until it reaches firm ball stage again. Remove pan from heat and stir in vanilla and pecans; mix well. Pour into buttered pan. When firm, turn out onto cutting board on wax paper. Cut caramel in 1-inch squares and wrap in plastic wrap. Makes 5 dozen.

Leona's Fudge

4 C. white sugar
1 (14½ oz.) can evaporated milk
¼ lb. butter
12 oz. pkg. chocolate chips

1 pt. jar marshmallow creme
1 tsp. vanilla
Nuts (opt.)

Cook to soft ball stage and sugar, evaporated milk and butter, stirring constantly. Remove from heat and immediately stir in chocolate chips, marshmallow creme and vanilla. Add nuts and pour at once in 9×13-inch buttered pan. Cut when cooled.

Good Times Fudge

4 C. sugar
1 large can evaporated milk
⅓ C. butter
Dash of salt
1 (12 oz.) pkg. chocolate chips

2 tsp. vanilla
1 C. chopped nuts
1 pt. marshmallow creme or
    16 marshmallows (cut-up fine) or
    2 C. miniature marshmallows

Combine sugar, evaporated milk, butter and salt. Boil til soft ball is formed, stirring constantly. Remove from heat. Add chocolate chips and beat. Add vanilla, nuts and marshmallows. Beat for 5 minutes and pour into a large buttered pan.

Grandma's Chocolate Fudge

2 C. sugar
1 C. milk
1/8 lb. butter
12-15 marshmallows (cut-up)

1 (6 oz.) pkg. chocolate chips
½ C. nuts
1 tsp. vanilla
½-1 sq. chocolate (opt.)

Stir sugar and milk together; add butter and bring to a boil, stirring frequently or constantly. Reduce heat and let boil until softball stage, stirring ccasionally. Drop in the marshmallows, chocolate chips, nuts and add the vanilla. Add the extra chocolate if you desire a more pronounced chocolate flavor. Stir until everything is melted and pour in oiled pan. Cool and cut in squares.

Brown Sugar Fudge

2 C. brown sugar
1 C. white sugar
1 C. light cream

½ C. butter
1 tsp. vanilla
1 C. chopped nuts

Combine sugars, cream and butter. Cook to softball stage (238°), stirring frequently; add vanilla. Cool to lukewarm (110°). Beat till mixture loses its gloss. Stir in nuts and pour into buttered 10×6×1½-inch pan. Cool and cut in squares.

Peanut Butter Popcorn Balls

1 C. raw popcorn	*1 C. chunky peanut butter*
1 C. white sugar	*1 tsp. vanilla*
1 C. light syrup	*1 C. Spanish salted peanuts (opt.)*

Pop corn and keep warm in 200° oven. Bring sugar and syrup to a rolling boil, stirring constantly. Remove from heat. Add peanut butter and vanilla; mix well. Pour over popcorn and mix well. Form into small balls. OPTIONAL: Add 1 C. peanuts to sryup mixture before pouring over popcorn.

Two-Layered Fudge

2¼ C. sugar	*1 tsp. vanilla*
¼ C. butter or margarine	*½ C. chocolate chips*
16 large marshmallows	*1 C. nuts*
¼ tsp. salt	*½ C. butterscotch chips*
1 C. evaporated milk	

Mix in a heavy saucepan the sugar, butter, marshmallow, salt and evaporated milk. Stir over medium heat until mixture boils and is bubbly all over top. Boil and stir over medium heat for 5 minutes more. Remove from heat and stir in vanilla. Pour half of mixture in a heat proof bowl. To one half add chocolate chips and nuts. To the other half add the butterscotch chips. Stir each batch until chips are dissolved and you have a creamy mixture. Spread chocolate mixture in a buttered square pan. Spread butterscotch mixture over top. Place in refrigerator until set.

Caramel Treats

1 (16 oz.) pkg. caramels
2 sticks oleo
1 can Bordens evaporated milk

Marshmallows
Rice Krispies

Melt caramels and oleo in double boiler. When melted, add 1 can of sweetened milk. Put toothpicks in marshmallows and freeze, then dip in caramel and roll in Rice Krispies.

Pumpkin Squares

1 (No. 1) can pumpkin (2 C.)
1 C. sugar
1 C. chopped, toasted pecans
½ gal. softened vanilla ice cream
36 gingersnaps

1 tsp. salt
1 tsp. ginger
1 tsp. cinnamon
½ tsp. nutmeg

Combine pumpkin, sugar, spices; add nuts. Fold pumpkin mixture into ice cream in a chilled bowl. Line bottom of 9×13-inch pan with half the gingersnaps; top with half the ice cream mixture, then another layer gingersnaps, remaining ice cream. Freeze until firm (5 hours or more). Cut into squares. Garnish with whipped cream of Dream Whip and pecan half.

"Just For Notes"

MISCELLANEOUS

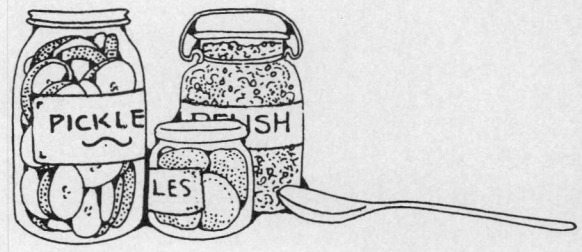

Miscellaneous

Smokey Salmon Spread

7½ oz. can salmon
8 oz. pkg. cream cheese (softened)

3 drops liquid smoke flavoring
3 T. sliced green onion

Drain salmon, save 2 tsp. liquid. Flake salmon. Combine cheese, liquied smoke and salmon liquid. Blend thoroughly, stir in onion. Fold in salmon. Refrigerate 2 hours or overnight for better flavor. Yield: 1½ C.

Cheese Loaf

1 lb. loaf Velveeta cheese
4 oz. Philadelphia cream cheese

1 medium onion (finely chopped)
¼ C. finely chopped pecans

Have cheese at room temperature. Mix all together with hands and shape into rolls (circumference of Ritz crackers). Roll on waxed paper which has been generously sprinkled with chili powder and paprika. Chill.

Wow Frosting

1 small box instant pudding
1 C. milk

¼ C. powdered sugar

Beat and let stand 5 minutes. Mix in small Extra Creamy Cool Whip.

Apple Oatmeal Pudding

3 C. sliced apples
½ C. sugar
1 T. flour
1/8 tsp. salt
1/8 tsp. cinnamon
½ C. brown sugar

½ C. flour
½ C. raw oatmeal
1/8 tsp. salt
1/8 tsp. baking powder
¼ C. butter

Combine sliced apples, sugar, flour, salt and cinnamon. Place in baking dish. Crumble with fingers the brown sugar, flour, oatmeal, salt, baking powder and butter. Put on top of first layer and bake at 350° for 30-40 minutes or until apples are tender.

Hot Chocolate Syrup

1 C. sugar
1/3 C. cocoa
1 T. butter

2 T. corn syrup
½ tsp. vanilla
1/8 tsp. salt

Melt butter in pan; add cocoa and stir over low heat until melted. Add boiling water gradually. Add sugar and syrup. Cook for 5 minutes, stirring often. Add vanilla and salt. Very good on ice cream.

Hot Mustard Sauce

Equal parts of sugar, flour and dried mustard. Moisten with vinegar.

Boaters' Snack Cheese Spread

1 lb. cheese (shredded)
1 large can evaporated milk
4 T. margarine

1 T. (scant) dry mustard
1 dash Tabasco sauce

Mix all together and heat in a double boiler until thoroughly blended. Makes approximately 3 pints. Store in refrigerator.

Pineapple Chutney

¾ C. sugar
½ C. cider vinegar
2 T. grated gingerroot
½ tsp. ground cumin
1/8 tsp. salt

1 C. coarsely chopped onion
¾ C. dried apricots (ea. quartered)
½ C. dark seedless raisins
1 fresh pineapple (coarsely chopped)

In 2-qt. pan, combine sugar, vinegar, gingerroot, cimin and salt. Heat to boiling over high heat. Stir in onions, apricots and raisins. Reheat to boiling, reduce to a simmer for 5 minutes. Cool to room temperature. Peel and quarter pineapple. Remove "eyes" and discard core. Coarsely chop fruit. In medium-size bowl, combine pineapple and cooled vinegar mixture. Cover tightly and refrigerate overnight. Serve with poultry or pork.

Horseradish Sauce

8 oz. cream cheese
1 T. powdered sugar
1 T. lemon juice

1 T. Worcestershire sauce
4 T. horseradish (any kind)
½ C. heavy cream

Soften cream cheese at room temperature. Blend in sugar, lemon juice, Worcestershire sauce and horseradish. Fold in heavy cream which has been whipped. Refrigerate. (Great on prime rib.)

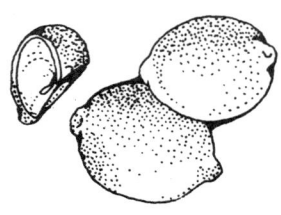

Casserole Sauce Mix

2 C. nonfat dry milk powder
¾ C. cornstarch
¼ C. powdered chicken bouillon
4 tsp. onion powder

1 tsp. dried thyme leaves
1 tsp. dried basil leaves
½ tsp. pepper

Use with chicken, tuna, macaroni and cheese. ¾ C. to a casserole.

Meat Sauce

1 onion
1 lb. hamburger
Red pepper
Sweet basil

1 clove garlic
1 (No. 2½) can tomatoes
1 can tomato paste

Chop onion. Cook in olive oil. Add hamburger. Cook until brown. Add rest of ingredients. Cook 2 hours.

Spicy Barbeque Sauce

½ C. honey
¼ C. lemon juice
3-4 T. low sodium soy sauce
2 T. steak sauce (opt.)

1 tsp. dry mustard
1 tsp. ground ginger
1/8 tsp. ground cloves

Mix in small saucepan. Bring to a boil and remove from heat. Makes about 1 C.

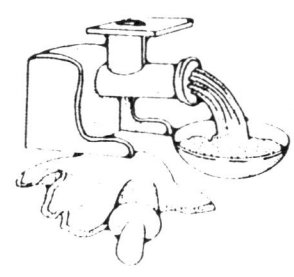

Refrigerator Pickles

4 C. sugar
½ C. salt
1½ tsp. celery seed
Cucumbers (thinly sliced)

4 C. vinegar
1½ tsp. turmeric
1½ tsp. mustard seed
3 large onions (thinly sliced)

Mix all ingredients except cucumbers and onions. Do not heat. Place cucumbers and onions in a covered container Pour brine over them. Refrigerate. Wait at least 5 days before using.

Easy Jam

1 C. strawberries or raspberries
1 C. sugar

1 tsp. lemon juice (opt.)

Crush enough berries to make 1 C., add 1 C. sugar and lemon juice. Boil hard for about 1 minute, check by raising spoon - when it coats spoon or form drops on bottom, it has cooked enough. If you want a firmer jam, you can cook it longer. Fresh or frozen fruit can be used. Never double recipe.

Crab Apple Pickles

1 gal. apples (washed and pricked)
5 C. sugar
4 C. dark vinegar
3 C. water

2 sticks cinnamon
1 T. whole allspice
½ T. whole cloves
Gauze bag

In large kettle mix sugar, vinegar and water. Tie spices in gauze bag and add to syrup mixture. Bring syrup to a boil and cook until sugar dissolves. Remove from heat and cool. When cooled add apples (whole) and return to heat. Simmer until apples are tender but not mushy. Remove from heat and let stand 12-18 hours. Remove apples from syrup and pack into hot jars. Heat syrup and pour over apples, seal with hot lids.

Helen's Dill Dandies

2 C. white vinegar
6 C. water

⅓ C. (scant) canning salt
Garlic cloves

Bring vinegar, salt and water to a boil. Pour into cucumber packed jars that have 2 garlic cloves also included. Let seal.

Sweet Pickles

2 C. vinegar
1 C. water
1½ T. mixed spices

1 T. grated horseradish
2 tsp. salt
2 T. alum

Wash cucumbers small or medium size and put into jars. Add vinegar, water, spices, horseradish, salt and alum. Seal with 2 piece lids, in cold packer filled with cold water. When water comes to a boil, turn off and let cool in water. When ready to use, wash cucumbers, after draining off spice mixture. Cut into disired size, add 2½ C. white sugar and let stand at least 24 hours before using. Makes its own syrup. Enough for 2 qts., if you need more liquid to fill jars, add extra vinegar to cover cucumbers.

Sweet Pickles

8 qts. cucumbers
½ C. pickling salt
4 C. vinegar
8 C. sugar

1 tsp. turmeric
1 T. celery seed
1 T. mixed pickling spice

Wash cucumbers. Place in a crock. Pour boiling water over them; let stand overnight. Drain and repeat for 6 days. On 7th day, drain; add salt. Cover with boiling water; let stand overnight. Drain. Prick cucumber or slice larger ones. Combine vinegar, 4 C. sugar, turmeric, celery seeds and pickling spices. Heat and pour over cucumbers, each morning for two or more mornings. Pack pickles in jars. Add remaining sugar to mixture, heat to boiling and pour over pickles in the jar and seal. (Do not use softened water, as this will shrivel cucumbers!)

Easy Dill Pickles

9 C. water
1 C. salt

2 C. vinegar
Dill

Combine ingredients. Put on stove and heat until bubbly. Do not boil. Put plenty of dill in jar, then pour over baby cucumbers. Put seal on, let set for couple of weeks, ready to eat. Boil lid in water before putting on jar.

Bread 'N Butter Pickles

1 qt. cider vinegar
1 pt. water
4 C. sugar
⅔ C. salt
Onions

2 tsp. celery seed
2 tsp. mustard seed
⅔ tsp. turmeric
½ tsp. ginger
Large cucumbers

Slice cucumbers in bowl, cover tightly. Refrigerate overnight. Then next day, fill jars with sliced cucumbers. Top with several slices of onion. Mix vinegar, water, sugar, salt, celery seed, mustard seed, turmeric and ginger into a large pan. Bring to boil and boil until sugar and salt dissolve. Pour sauce over cucumber until they are covered. If using rubbers and zinc lids, wipe jar off and put lids on and tighten. This is all you have to do to seal these jars. If using flats and bands, wipe jar off, put lids on and tighten. Bring ¾ full canner of water to boil. Add jars and boil for 5 minutes. Remove jars and tighten lids if necessary. Let all jars stand for 6 weeks before using to allow flavors to completely penetrate the cucumbers. Makes 3½-4 quarts.

Cinnamon Pickles

2 gallons cucumbers

8½ qts. water

Let stand 24 hours. Drain and rinse. Soak 3 hours in cold water. Drain well.

In a large kettle:
1 bottle red food color
1 T. alum

1 C. vinegar
Water to cover cucumbers

Add cucumbers and simmer 2 hours. Drain.

SYRUP:
2 C. vinegar
2 C. water

10 C. sugar
1 pkg. cinnamon candies or
red hots

Pour hot over cucumbers overnight. Repeat 3 days. On third day pack in jars. Pour hot syrup over and seal.

Zucchini Jam

5½ C. grated zucchini
6 C. sugar
1 C. water
2 T. lemon juice

1 (20 oz.) can crushed pineapple
2 (3 oz. ea.) pkgs. Jello
(any flavor)

Boil 6 minutes zucchini, sugar and water. Add lemon juice and pineapple. Boil 6 minutes more. Add two 3 oz. each pkgs. Jello. Boil 6 minutes more. Pour hot mixture into jars, put on lid and screw band. Jars will seal without processing if you put on lids immediately after you pour in hot mixture.

Easy Strawberry Jam

1 qt. fresh or frozen strawberries
1 T. butter

4 C. sugar
2 T. lemon juice

In Dutch oven size pan, combine strawberries with 2 C. sugar. Bring to boil over medium-high heat. Boil for 2 minutes. Add 2 C. more sugar and 1 T. butter. Bring back to boil and boil for 3 minutes. Mixture will boil to top of pan. Stir occasionally while cooking. Take off of heat and add lemon juice. Let stand, stirring occasionally until cold. Skim off white film on top. Put in containers and freeze. Keeps well for up to 1 year.

Need A Gift?

For

- **Shower** • **Birthday** • **Mother's Day** •
  • **Anniversary** • **Christmas** •

Turn Page for Order Form
(Order Now While Supply Lasts!)

To Order Copies Of

Lake Country Cookbook

Please send me _____ copies of **Lake Country Cookbook** at $11.95 each. (Make checks payable to **QUIXOTE PRESS**.)

Name _____

Street _____

City _____State _____Zip _____

Send Orders To:
Quixote Press
R.R. #4, Box 33B • Blvd. Station
Sioux City, Iowa 51109

- -

To Order Copies Of

Lake Country Cookbook

Please send me _____ copies of **Lake Country Cookbook** at $11.95 each. (Make checks payable to **QUIXOTE PRESS**.)

Name _____

Street _____

City _____State _____Zip _____

Send Orders To:
Quixote Press
R.R. #4, Box 33B • Blvd. Station
Sioux City, Iowa 51109

STANDARD ABBREVIATIONS

tsp. - teaspoon
T. - tablespoon
C. - cup
f.g. - few grains
pt. - pint
qt. - quart

d.b. - double boiler
B.P. - baking powder
oz. - ounce
lb. - pounds
pk. - peck
bu. - bushel

GUIDE TO WEIGHTS AND MEASURES

1 teaspoon - 60 drops
3 teaspoons - 1 tablespoon
2 tablespoons - 1 fluid ounce
4 tablespoons - 1/4 cup
5 1/3 tablespoons - 1/3 cup
8 tablespoons - 1/2 cup
16 tablespoons - 1 cup

1 pound - 16 ounces
1 cup - 1/2 pint
2 cups - 1 pint
4 cups - 1 quart
4 quarts - 1 gallon
8 quarts - 1 peck
4 pecks - 1 bushel

SUBSTITUTIONS AND EQUIVALENTS

2 tablespoons of fat - 1 ounce
1 cup of fat - 1/2 pound
1 pound of butter -2 cups
1 cup of hydrogenated fat plus 1/2 t. salt - 1 cup butter
2 cups sugar - 1 pound
2 1/2 cups packed brown sugar - 1 pound
1 1/3 cups packed brown sugar - 1 cup of granulated sugar
3 1/2 cups of powdered sugar - 1 pound
4 cups sifted all-purpose flour - 1 pound
4 1/2 cups sifted cake flour - 1 pound
1 ounce bitter chocolate - 1 square
4 tablespoons cocoa plus 2 teaspoon butter - 1 ounce of bitter chocolate
1 cup egg whites - 8 to 10 whites
1 cup egg yolks - 12 to 14 yolks
16 marshmallows - 1/4 pound
1 tablespoon cornstarch - 2 tablespoons flour for thickening
1 tablespoon vinegar or lemon juice + 1 cup milk - 1 cup sour milk
10 graham crackers - 1 cup fine crumbs
1 cup whipping cream - 2 cups whipped
1 cup evaporated milk - 3 cups whipped
1 lemon - 3 to 4 tablespoons juice
1 orange - 6 to 8 tablespoons juice
1 cup uncooked rice - 3 to 4 cups cooked rice

SUBSTITUTIONS

FOR	YOU CAN USE. . .
1 T. cornstarch	2 T. flour OR 1½ T. quick cooking tapioca
1 C. cake flour	1 C. less 2 T. all-purpose flour
1 C. all-purpose flour	1 C. plus 2 T. cake flour
1 sq. chocolate	3 T. cocoa & 1 T. fat
1 C. melted shortening	1 C. salad oil (may not be substituted for solid shortening)
1 C. milk	½ C. evaporated milk & ½ C. water
1 C. sour milk or buttermilk	1 T. lemon juice or vinegar & enough sweet milk to measure 1 C.
1 C. heavy cream	⅔ C. milk & ⅓ C. butter
Sweetened condensed milk	No substitution
1 egg	2 T. dried whole egg & 2 T. water
1 tsp. baking powder	¼ tsp. baking soda & 1 tsp. cream of tartar OR ¼ tsp. baking soda & ½ C. sour milk, buttermilk or molasses; reduce other liquid ½ C.
1 C. sugar	1 C. honey; reduce other liquid ¼ C.; reduce baking temperature by 25°
1 C. miniature marshmallows	About 10 large marshmallows (cut-up)
1 medium onion (2½-inch diameter)	2 T. instant minced onion OR 1 tsp. onion powder OR 2 T. onion salt; reduce salt 1 tsp.
1 garlic clove	1/8 tsp. garlic powder OR ¼ tsp. garlic salt; reduce salt 1/8 tsp.
1 T. fresh herbs	1 tsp. dried herbs OR ¼ tsp. powdered herbs OR ½ tsp. herb salt; reduce salt ¼ tsp.

Protein Content and Caloric Value of Foods for Your Diet

Food	Oz.	Approximate Measure	Protein	Calories
Lamb				
Chops				
Loin or				
rib	4	1 loin or 2 rib 1-inch thick	17.9	421
Shoulder	4	Piece 4x3x5/8-inch	18.7	348
Roasts				
Leg	4	Slice 4x3x½-inch	21.6	276
Shoulder	4	Slice 5x3x½-inch	18.7	348
Pork, fresh				
Chops and steaks				
Leg (ham)	4	Piece 3½x3x½-inch	18.2	408
Loin	4	Chop ¾-inch thick	19.7	349
Shoulder	4	Piece 4½x3½x3/8-inch	16.1	464
Roasts				
Boston butt	4	Slice 4½x3½x3/8-inch	19.9	327
Loin	4	Slice ¾-inch thick	19.7	349
Tenderloin	4	2 pieces 1-inch dia.x3-inches long	23.9	172
Pork, cured				
Bacon,				
Canadian				
style	1	Slice 2¼-inch diameter by 3/16-inch thick	6.6	68
Ham				
(boiled)	2	Slice 4¼x4x1/8-inch	10.6	147
Veal				
Chops				
Loin	4	Chop 5/8-inch thick	23.0	211
Rib	4	Chop ¾-inch thick	22.6	241
Roasts				
Leg	4	Slice 4x2½x½-inch	22.9	223
Loin	4	Slice 4x2½x½-inch	23.0	211
Rib	4	Slice 4x2½x½-inch	22.6	241
Shoulder	4	Slice 5x3x½-inch	23.3	202
Steaks				
Cutlet				
(round)	4	Piece 4x2½x½-inch	23.4	191
Shoulder	4	Piece 5x3x½-inch	23.3	202
Sirloin	4	Piece 4x2½x½-inch	23.0	211
Stew				
(breast)	4	4 pieces 2½x1x1-inch	22.0	271
Variety Meats				
Brains (beef)	4	2 pieces 2½x1½x1-inch	12.6	152
Heart (avg.)	4	⅓ ht. 3-inch dia. x 3½-inch long	19.7	157
Kidney (avg.)	4	3 slices 3¼x2½x¼-inch	20.0	161
Liver				
Beef	3	2 slices 3x2½x3/8-inch	17.7	119
Lamb	3	2 slices 3½x2x3/8-inch	18.9	118
Pork	3	2 slices 3½x2x3/8-inch	17.7	116
Veal	3	2 slices 3x2½x3/8-inch	17.1	122
Sweetbread	4	Piece 4x3x¾-inch	18.2	216
Tongue	3	3 slices 3x2x¼-inch	15.7	191

Protein Content and Caloric Value of Foods for Your Diet

Food	Oz.	Approximate Measure	Protein	Calories
Sausages and Cooked Specialties				
Bologna	1	Slice 4½ dia. x ½-inch thick	4.4	65
Frankfurter	2	2 5½-inch long x ¾-inch dia.	9.1	121
Liver sausage	1	Slice 3-inch dia. x ¼-inch thick	5.0	77
Luncheon meat	1	Slice 4x3½x1/8-inch	4.6	81
Vienna sausage	1	2 pieces 2-inch long x ¾-inch diameter	5.8	76
Poultry				
Chicken				
Liver	3	4 avg.	19.9	122
Roast				
Breast	3	½ breast	21.0	110
Leg	2½	1 avg.	14.7	88
Thigh	2½	1 avg.	15.8	95
Wing	1	1 avg.	7.0	37
Stewed				
Dark meat	3½	½ cup (diced)	23.1	139
Light meat	3	½ cup (diced)	20.3	106
Turkey				
Roast				
Dark meat	3½	Slice 4x3x½-inch	23.2	177
Light meat	3½	Slice 4x3x½-inch	24.5	139
Fish				
Bass	4	1 small fish	27.3	113
Clams	3½	5 medium	12.8	77
Cod	3½	Piece 4x2¼x¾-inch	16.5	70
Crab (canned)	3	⅔ cup	16.1	94
Finnan haddie	3½	¾ cup	23.2	96
Flounder	3½	Piece 4x3x3/8-inch	19.0	79
Haddock	3½	Piece 3½x3x¾-inch	17.2	72
Halibut	4	Piece 4x3x½-inch	20.4	133
Herring, fresh	4	1 fish 7-inches long	22.8	163
Lobster				
Canned	3	½ cup	15.6	74
Fresh	2½	1 avg.	12.2	63
Mackerel	2½	¼ fish 7-inches long	14.3	119
Oysters	3½	5 medium	6.0	50
Perch	4	2 fish 4½-inches long	23.4	102
Salmon				
Canned	3½	⅔ cup	24.7	203
Fresh	3	Piece 2½x2½x7/8-inch	15.7	196
Shrimp (canned)	2	3/8 cup or 12 pieces 1-inch dia.	10.7	49
Trout	3	Piece 6-inches long	16.1	80
White fish	4	Piece 3¼-inchx3x½-inch	25.2	165
Milk and Dairy Products				
Butter	⅓		.1	73
Cheese, cottage	2	¼ cup	9.6	51
Cream, coffee	½	1 T.	.4	29

Protein Content and Caloric Value of Foods for Your Diet

Food	Approx. Weight (Oz.)	Approximate Measure (Gm.)	Protein	Calories
Milk				
Buttermilk	7	1 glass	7.0	72
Evaporated	4	½ cup	8.4	167
Skim	7	1 glass	7.0	72
Whole	7	1 glass	7.0	138
Eggs	1²⁄₃	1 medium	6.4	79
Potatoes				
White	2	1 small 2½-inch long x 2-inch dia.	1.2	51
Vegetables				
Artichokes	3½	½ large	2.9	63
Asparagus	3½	7 stalks 6-inches long	2.3	27
Beans, string	3½	²⁄₃ cup	2.4	42
Beet greens	3½	½ cup	2.0	33
Beets	3½	²⁄₃ cup or 2 1¾-inch dia.	1.6	46
Broccoli	3½	2 stalks 5-inches long	3.3	37
Brussels sprts.	3½	²⁄₃ cup	4.4	58
Cabbage	3½	1/5 head 4½-inch dia.	1.4	29
Carrots	3½	2 carrots 5-inch long	1.2	45
Cauliflower	3½	²⁄₃ cup	2.4	31
Celery	½	Piece 8½-inch long or 2 hts.	.2	3
Chard, Swiss	3½	½ cup	1.4	25
Chicory	1	10 small leaves	.4	7
Cucumbers	2	8 slices 1/8-inch thick	.4	7
Eggplant	2	Slices 3½-inch dia x 3/8-inch thick	.7	17
Endive, French	2	2 stalks	.8	11
Green pepper	½	½ cup or piece 4x1¾-inch	.2	4
Kohlrabi	3½	²⁄₃ cup (diced)	2.1	36
Lettuce				
Head	3½	¼ head 4-inch diameter	1.2	18
	½	1 leaf	.2	3
Leaf	½	2 leaves	.1	2
Mushrooms	3½	5 caps 2¼-inch dia.	2.6	15
Okra	2	5 pods	1.0	21
Onions				
Dried	3	1 onion 2-inch dia.	1.2	42
Green	½	3 medium	.2	7
Parsley		2 sprigs	.1	1
Pumpkin	3½	½ cup	1.2	36
Radishes	1	3 radishes 1-inch dia.	.4	7
Rutabagas	3½	½ cup	1.1	41
Sauerkraut	3½	²⁄₃ cup	1.1	18
Spinach	3½	¾ cup	2.3	25
Squash				
Summer	3½	½ cup	.6	19
Winter	3½	½ cup	1. 5	44
Tomatoes				
Canned	3½	½ cup	1.2	25
Fresh	3½	1 tomato 2-inch dia.	1.0	23
Juice, canned	4	½ cup	1.2	28
Turnip greens	3½	½ cup	2.9	37

Protein Content and Caloric Value of Foods for Your Diet

Food	Oz.	Approximate Measure	Protein	Calories
Turnips				
White	3½	⅔ cup	1.1	35
Yellow (see	rutabagas)			
Pickles				
Olives				
Green	1/6	1 medium	.1	7
Ripe	½	1 large	.2	23
Pickles				
Dill	2	½ pickle 5-inches long x1½-inch diameter	.3	7
Sweet	½	1 pickle 2½-inches long x¾-inch diameter	.2	21

BREAD AND CEREAL PRODUCTS

Food	Oz.	Approximate Measure	Protein	Calories
Cereals				
Bran, whole	⅔	⅓ cup	2.5	67
Cornflakes	½	⅔ cup	1.3	56
Farina, enriched	⅔	½ cup (sc. 2 T. dry)	2.3	71
Oatmeal	⅔	½ cup (¼ cup dry)	3.1	77
Rice				
Puffed	⅓	¾ cup	.7	36
White	1	⅔ cup (2 T. dry)	2.3	105
Wheat				
Flakes	⅔	¾ cup	2.4	74
Puffed	⅓	¾ cup	1.2	37
Shredded	1	1 biscuit	2.9	103
Breads				
Rye	⅔	Slice 4x3½x½-inch	1.2	50
Wheat				
Melba toast	1/6	Slice 3x2x¼-inch	.6	19
White, enrch	⅔	1 slice (commercial) thin	1.6	50
Whole wheat	⅔	1 slice (commercial) thin	1.8	50
Crackers				
Graham	½	1 cracker 3-inch square	1.0	54
Saltine	½	1 cracker 2-inch square	.4	17
Soda	1/5	1 cracker 2¾x2½-inch	.6	25
Zwieback	¼	1 piece 3¼x1¼x½-inch	.9	33

Beverages

Food	Oz.	Approximate Measure	Protein	Calories
Carbonated	6	1 small bottle		82
Coffee, black			0	0
Tea, plain			0	0

Fruits

Food	Oz.	Approximate Measure	Protein	Calories
Apples	3½	1 apple 2¼-inch diameter	.3	65
Apricots	1	1 medium	.4	20
Blackberries	3½	¾ cup	1.2	62
Blueberries	3½	⅔ cup	.6	68
Cantaloupe	4	¼ melon 5-inch diameter	.8	29
Cherries, sweet	3½	15 cherries 7/8-inch diameter	1.2	87
Grapefruit	3½	½ medium 3 5/8-inch dia.	.5	44
Grapes				
Concord	3½	34 avg.	1.4	78
Green seedless	3½	40 small	.8	74
Malaga or Tokay	3½	21 avg.	.8	74

Protein Content and Caloric Value of Foods for Your Diet

Honeydew melon	4	1½-inch slice, 7-inch melon	.9	48
Oranges	3½	½ orange 4-inch diameter	.9	52
Peaches	3½	1 medium	.5	51
Pears	3½	1 small	.7	70
Pineapple	3½	1 slice 4-inch diameter x ½-inch thick	.4	58
Plums	2½	1 plum 1¾-inch dia.	.5	39
Raspberries	3	⅔ cup	1.1	64
Strawberries	3½	10 strawberries 1-inch dia.	.8	41
Watermelon	5	½ slice 6-inch dia. x ¾-inch thick	.8	51
FRUIT JUICES				
Grapefruit, canned	4	½ cup	.6	49
Orange	4	½ cup	.7	66
Pineapple canned	4	½ cup	.4	65
Tomato (see	vegetables)			

HOW MANY DROPS IN A "DASH"?
Here, a cook's guide to the most-often-called-for food measures and equivalents

How many cups of berries in a pint? How many slices of bread make a half cup of crumbs? For two tablespoons of orange peel, will you need more than one orange? You'll find the answers to these questions and lots more in this handy kitchen chart.

EQUIVALENT MEASURES

Dash	2 to 3 drops or less than 1/8 teaspoon
1 tablespoon	3 teaspoons
¼ cup	4 tablespoons
⅓ cup	5 tablespoons plus 1 teaspoon
½ cup	8 tablespoons
1 cup	16 tablespoons
1 pint	2 cups
1 quart	4 cups
1 gallon	4 quarts
1 peck	8 quarts
1 bushel	4 pecks
1 pound	16 ounces

FOOD EQUIVALENTS

Apples *1 pound*	3 medium (3 cups sliced)
Bananas *1 pound*	3 medium (1⅓ cups mashed)
Berries *1 pint*	1¾ cups
Bread *1 pound loaf*	14 to 20 slices
Bread crumbs, fresh *1 slice* bread with crust	½ cup bread crumbs
Broth, chicken or beef *1 cup*	1 bouillon cube or 1 envelope bouillon or 1 teaspoon instant bouillon dissolved in 1 cup boiling water
Butter or margarine *¼ pound stick*	½ cup
Cheese *¼ pound*	1 cup, shredded
Cheese, cottage *8 ounces*	1 cup
Cheese, cream *3 ounces*	6 tablespoons
Chocolate, unsweetened *1 ounce*	1 square
Chocolate, semi-sweet pieces *6 ounce package*	1 cup

QUANTITIES TO SERVE 100 PEOPLE

Coffee	—3 lbs.
Loaf Sugar	—3 lbs.
Cream	—3 qts.
Whipping Cream	—4 pts.
Milk	—6 gallons
Fruit	—2½ gallons
Fruit Juice	—4 (No. 10 ea.) cans (26 lbs.)
Tomato Juice	—4 (No. 10 ea.) cans (26 lbs.)
Soup	—5 gallons
Oysters	—18 qts.
Weiners	—25 lbs.
Meatloaf	—24 lbs.
Ham	—40 lbs.
Beef	—40 lbs.
Roast Pork	—40 lbs.
Hamburger	—30-36 lbs.
Chicken For Chicken Pie	—40 lbs.
Potatoes	—35 lbs.
Scalloped Potatoes	—5 gallon
Vegetables	—4 (No. 10 ea.) cans (26 lbs.)
Baked Beans	—5 gallon
Beets	—30 lbs.
Cauliflower	—18 lbs.
Cabbage For Slaw	—20 lbs.
Carrots	—33 lbs.
Bread	—10 loaves
Rolls	—200
Butter	—3 lbs.
Potato Salad	—12 qts.
Fruit Salad	—20 qts.
Vegetable Salad	—20 qts.
Lettuce	—20 heads
Salad Dressing	—3 qts.
Pies	—18
Cakes	—8
Ice Cream	—4 gallons
Cheese	—3 lbs.
Olives	—1¾ lbs.
Pickles	—2 qts.
Nuts	—3 lbs. sorted

To Serve 50 People, Divide by 2
To Serve 25 People, Divide by 4

THE KITCHEN
General Household Hints

SALT

If stew is too salty, add raw cut potatoes and discard once they have cooked and absorbed the salt. Another remedy is to add a teaspoon each of cider vinegar and sugar. Or, simply add sugar.

If soup or stew is too sweet, add salt. For a main dish or vegetable, add a teaspoon of cider vinegar.

GRAVY

For pale gravy, color with a few drops of Kitchen Bouquet. Or to avoid the problem in the first place, brown the flour well before adding the liquid. This also helps prevent lumpy gravy.

To make gravy smooth, keep a jar with a mixture of equal parts of flour and cornstarch. Put 3-4 T. of this mixture in another jar and add some water. Shake, and in a few minutes you will have a smooth paste for gravy.

To remedy greasy gravy, add a small amount of baking soda.

For quick thickener for gravies, add some instant potatoes to your gravy and it will thicken beautifully.

VEGETABLES

If fresh vegetables are wilted or blemished, pick off the brown edges. Sprinkle with cool water, wrap in towel and refrigerate for an hour or so.

Perk up soggy lettuce by adding lemon juice to a bowl of cold water and soak for an hour in the refrigerator.

Lettuce and celery will crisp up fast if you place it in a pan of cold water and add a few sliced potatoes.

If vegetables are overdone, put the pot in a pan of cold water. Let it stand from 15 minutes to ½ hour without scraping pan.

By lining the crisper section of your refrigerator with newspaper and wrapping vegetables with it, moisture will be absorbed and your vegetables will stay fresher longer.

EGGS

If you shake the egg and you hear a rattle, you can be sure it's stale. A really fresh egg will float and a stale one will sink.

If you are making deviled eggs and want to slice it perfectly, dip the knife in water first. The slice will be smooth with no yolk sticking to the knife.

The white of an egg is easiest to beat when it's at room temperature. So leave it out of the refrigerator about ½ hour before using it.

To make light and fluffy scrambled eggs, add a little water while beating the eggs.

Add vinegar to the water while boiling eggs. Vinegar helps to seal the egg, since it acts on the calcium in the shell.

To make quick-diced eggs, take your potato masher and go to work on a boiled egg.

If you wrap each egg in aluminum foil before boiling it, the shell won't crack when it's boiling.

To make those eggs go further when making scrambled eggs for a crowd, add a pinch of baking powder and 2 tsp. of water per egg.

A great trick for peeling eggs the easy way - when they are finished boiling, turn off the heat and just let them sit in the pan with the lid on for about 5 minutes. Steam will build up under the shell and they will just fall away.

Or, quickly rinse hot hard-boiled eggs in cold water, and the shells will be easier to remove.

When you have saved a lot of egg yolks from previous recipes; use them in place of whole eggs for baking or thickening. Just add 2 yolks for every whole egg.

Fresh or hard-boiled? Spin the egg. If it wobbles, it is raw - if it spins easily, it's hard-boiled.

Add a few drops of vinegar to the water when poaching an egg to keep it from running all over the pan.

Add 1 T. of water per egg white to increase the quantity of beaten egg white when making meringue.

Try adding eggshells to coffee after it has perked, for a better flavor.

POTATOES

Overcooked potatoes can become soggy when the milk is added. Sprinkle with dry powdered milk for the fluffiest mashed potatoes ever.

To hurry up baked potatoes, boil in salted water for 10 minutes, then place in a very hot oven. Or, cut potatoes in half and place them face down on a baking sheet in the oven to make the baking time shorter.

When making potato pancakes, add a little sour cream to keep potatoes from discoloring.

Save some of the water in which the potatoes were boiled - add to some powdered milk and use when mashing. This restores some of the nutrients that were lost in the cooking process.

Use a couple of tablespoons of cream cheese in place of butter for your potatoes; try using sour cream instead of milk when mashing.

ONIONS

To avoid tears when peeling onions, peel them under cold water or refrigerate before chopping.

For sandwiches to go in lunchboxes, sprinkle with dried onion. They will have turned into crisp pieces by lunchtime.

Peel and quarter onions. Place one layer deep in a pan and freeze. Quickly pack in bags or containers while frozen. Use as needed, chopping onions while frozen, with a sharp knife.

TOMATOES

Keep tomatoes in storage with stems pointed downward and they will retain their freshness longer.

Sunlight doesn't ripen tomatoes. It's the warmth that makes them ripen. So find a warm spot near the stove or dishwasher where they can get a little heat.

Save the juice from canned tomatoes in ice cube trays. When frozen, store in plastic bags in freezer for cooking use or for tomato drinks.

To improve the flavor of inexpensive tomato juice, pour a 46-ounce can of it into a refrigerator jar and add one chopped green onion and a cut-up stalk of celery.

ROCK-HARD BROWN SUGAR
Add a slice of soft bread to the package of brown sugar, close the bag tightly, and in a few hours the sugar will be soft again. If you need it in a hurry, simply grate the amount called for with a hand grater. Or, put brown sugar and a cup of water (do not add to the sugar, set it alongside of it) in a covered pan. Place in the oven (low heat) for awhile. Or, buy liquid brown sugar.

THAWING FROZEN MEAT
Seal the meat in a plastic bag and place in a bowl of very warm water. Or, put in a bag and let cold water run over it for an hour or so.

CAKED OR CLOGGED SALT
Tightly wrap a piece of aluminum foil around the salt shaker. This will keep the dampness out of the salt. To prevent clogging, keep 5 to 10 grains of rice inside your shaker.

SOGGY POTATO CHIPS, CEREAL AND CRACKERS
If potato chips lose their freshness, place under broiler for a few moments. Care must be taken not to brown them. You can crisp soggy cereal and crackers by putting them on a cookie sheet and heating for a few minutes in the oven.

PANCAKE SYRUP
To make an inexpensive syrup for pancakes, save small amounts of leftover jams and jellies in a jar. Or, fruit-flavored syrup can be made by adding 2 C. sugar to 1 C. of any kind of fruit juice and cooking until it boils.

EASY TOPPING
A good topping for gingerbread, coffeecake, etc., can easily be made by freezing the syrup from canned fruit and adding 1 T. of butter and 1 T. of lemon juice to 2 C. of syrup. Heat until bubbly, and thicken with 2 T. of flour.

TASTY CHEESE SANDWICHES
Toast cheese sandwiches in a frying pan lightly greased with bacon fat for a delightful new flavor.

HURRY-UP HAMBURGERS
Poke a hole in the middle of the patties while shaping them. The burgers will cook faster and the holes will disappear when done.

SHRINKLESS LINKS
Boil sausage links for about 8 minutes before frying and they will shrink less and not break at all. Or, you can roll them lightly in flour before frying.

FROZEN BREAD
Put frozen bread loaves in a clean brown paper bag and place for 5 minutes in a 325° oven to thaw completely.

REMOVING THE CORN SILK
Dampen a paper towel or terry cloth and brush downward on the cob of corn. Every strand should come off.

NUTS
To quickly crack open a large amount of nuts, put in a bag and gently hammer until they are cracked open. Then remove nutmeats with a pick.

If nuts are stale, place them in the oven at 250° and leave them there for 5 to 10 minutes. The heat will revive them.

PREVENTING BOIL-OVERS
Add a lump of butter or a few teaspoons of cooking oil to the water. Rice, noodles or spaghetti will not boil over or stick together.

SOFTENING BUTTER
Soften butter quickly by grating it. Or heat a small pan and place it upside-down over the butter dish for several minutes. Or place in the microwave for a few seconds.

MEASURING STICKY LIQUIDS
Before measuring honey or syrup, oil the cup with cooking oil and rinse in hot water.

SCALDED MILK
Add a bit of sugar (without stirring) to milk to prevent it from scorching.

Rinse the pan in cold water before scalding milk, and it will be much easier to clean.

TENDERIZING MEAT
Boiled meat: Add a tablespoon of vinegar to the cooking water.

Tough meat or game: Make a marinade of equal parts cooking vinegar and heated bouillon. Marinate for 2 hours.

Steak: Simply rub in a mixture of cooking vinegar and oil. Allow to stand for 2 hours.

Chicken: To stew an old hen, soak it in vinegar for several hours before cooking. It will taste like a spring chicken.

INSTANT WHITE SAUCE
Blend together 1 C. soft butter and 1 C. flour. Spread in an ice cube tray, chill well, cut into 16 cubes before storing in a plastic bag in the freezer. For medium-thick sauce, drop 1 cube into 1 C. of milk and heat slowly, stirring as it thickens.

UNPLEASANT COOKING ODORS
While cooking vegetables that give off unpleasant odors, simmer a small pan of vinegar on top of the stove. Or, add vinegar to the cooking water. To remove the odor of fish from cooking and serving implements, rinse in vinegar water.

DON'T LOSE THOSE VITAMINS
Put vegetables in water after the water boils - not before - to be sure to preserve all the vegetables' vitamins.

CLEAN AND DEODORIZE YOUR CUTTING BOARD
Bleach it clean with lemon juice. Take away strong odors like onion with baking soda. Just rub in.

KEEP THE COLOR IN BEETS
If you find that your beets tend to lose color when you boil them, add a little lemon juice.

NO-SMELL CABBAGE
Two things to do to keep cabbage smell from filling the kitchen; don't overcook it (keep it crisp) and put half a lemon in the water when you boil it.

A GREAT ENERGY SAVER
When you're near the end of the baking time, turn the oven off and keep the door closed. The heat will stay the same long enough to finish baking your cake or pie and you'll save all that energy.

GRATING CHEESE
Chill the cheese before grating and it will take much less time.

SPECIAL LOOKING PIES
Give a unique look to your pies by using pinking shears to cut the dough. Make a pinked lattice crust!

REMOVING HAM RIND
Before placing ham in the roasting pan, slit rind lengthwise on the underside. The rind will peel away as the ham cooks, and can be easily removed.

SLUGGISH CATSUP
Push a drinking straw to the bottom of the bottle and remove. This admits enough air to start the catsup flowing.

UNMOLDING GELATIN
Rinse the mold pan in cold water and coat with salad oil. The oil will give the gelatin a nice luster and it will easily fall out of the mold.

LEFTOVER SQUASH
Squash that is leftover can be improved by adding some maple syrup before reheated.

NO-SPILL CUPCAKES
An ice cream scoop can be used to fill cupcake papers without spilling.

SLICING CAKE OR TORTE
Use dental floss to slice evenly and cleanly through a cake or torte - simply stretch a length of the floss taut and press down through the cake.

CANNING PEACHES
Don't bother to remove skins when canning or freezing peaches. They will taste better and be more nutritious with the skin on.

ANGEL FOOD COOKIES
Stale angel food cake can be cut into ½-inch slices and shaped with cookie cutters to make delicious "cookies". Just toast in the oven for a few minutes.

HOW TO CHOP GARLIC
Chop in a small amount of salt to prevent pieces from sticking to the knife or chopping board then pulverize with the tip or the knife.

EXCESS FAT ON SOUPS OR STEWS
Remove fat from stews or soups by refrigerating and eliminating fat as it rises and hardens on the surface. Or add lettuce leaves to the pot - the fat will cling to them. Discard lettuce before serving.

BROILED MEAT DRIPPINGS
Place a piece of bread under the rack on which you are broiling meat. Not only will this absorb the dripping fat, but it will reduce the chance of the fat catching on fire.

FAKE SOUR CREAM
To cut down on calories, run cottage cheese through the blender. It can be flavored with chives, extracts, etc., and used in place of mayonnaise.

BROWNED BUTTER
Browning brings out the flavor of the butter, so only half as much is needed for seasoning vegetables if it is browned before it is added.

COOKING DRIED BEANS
When cooking dried beans, add salt after cooking; if salt is added at the start it will slow the cooking process.

TASTY CARROTS
Adding sugar and horseradish to cooked carrots improves their flavor.

CARROT MARINADE
Marinate carrot sticks in dill pickle juice.

CLEAN CUKES
A ball of nylon net cleans and smooths cucumbers when making pickles.

FRESH GARLIC
Peel garlic and store in a covered jar of vegetable oil. The garlic will stay fresh and the oil will be nicely flavored for salad dressings.

LEFTOVER WAFFLES
Freeze waffles that are left; they can be reheated in the toaster.

FLUFFY RICE
Rice will be fluffier and whiter if you add 1 tsp. of lemon juice to each quart of water.

NUTRITIOUS RICE
Cook rice in liquid saved from cooking vegetables to add flavor and nutrition. A nutty taste can be achieved by adding wheat germ to the rice.

PERFECT NOODLES
When cooking noodles, bring required amount of water to a boil, add noodles, turn heat off and allow to stand for 20 minutes. This prevents overboiling and the chore of stirring. Noodles won't stick to the pan with this method.

EASY CROUTONS
Make delicious croutons for soup or salad by saving toast, cutting into cubes, and sauteeing in garlic butter.

BAKED FISH
To keep fish from sticking to the pan, bake on a bed of chopped onion, celery and parsley. This also adds a nice flavor to the fish.

NON-STICKING BACON
Roll a package of bacon into a tube before opening. This will loosen the slices and keep them from sticking together.

TASTY HOT DOGS
Boil hot dogs in sweet pickle juice and a little water for a different tate.

GOLDEN-BROWN CHICKEN
For golden-brown fried chicken, roll it in powdered milk instead of flour.

DOUBLE BOILER HINT
Toss a few marbles in the bottom of a double boiler. When the water boils down, the noise will let you know!

FLOUR PUFF
Keep a powder puff in your flour container to easily dust your rolling pin or pastry board.

JAR LABELS
Attach canning labels to the lids instead of the sides of jelly jars, to prevent the chore of removing the labels when the contents are gone.

DIFFERENT MEATBALLS
Try using crushed corn flakes or corn bread instead of bread crumbs in a meatball recipe or use onion-flavored potato chips.

CLEAN-UP TIPS

APPLIANCES
To rid yellowing from white appliances try this. Mix together ½ C. bleach, ¼ C. baking soda, and 4 C. warm water. Apply with a sponge and let set for 10 minutes. Rinse and dry thoroughly.

Instead of using commercial waxes, shine with rubbing alcohol.

For quick clean-ups, rub with equal parts water and household ammonia.

Or, try club soda. It cleans and polishes at the same time.

BLENDER
Fill part way with hot water and add a drop of detergent. Cover and turn it on for a few seconds. Rinse and drain dry.

BREADBOARDS
To rid cutting board of onion, garlic or fish smell, cut a lime or lemon in two and rub the surface with the cut side of the fruit.

Or, make a paste of baking soda and water and apply generously. Rinse.

COPPER POTS
Fill a spray bottle with vinegar and add 3 T. of salt. Spray solution liberally on copper pot. Let set for awhile, then simply rub clean.

Dip lemon halves in salt and rub.

Or, rub with Worcestershire sauce or catsup. The tarnish will disappear.

Clean with toothpaste and rinse.

BURNT AND SCORCHED PANS
Sprinkle burnt pans liberally with baking soda, adding just enough water to moisten. Let stand for several hours. You can generally lift the burned portions right out of the pan.

Stubborn stains on non-stick cookware can be removed by boiling 2 T. of baking soda, ½ C. vinegar, and 1 C. water for 10 minutes. Re-season with salad oil.

CAST-IRON SKILLETS
Clean the outside of the pan with commercial oven cleaner. Let set for 2 hours and the accumulated black stains can be removed with vinegar and water.

CAN OPENER
Loosen grime by brushing with an old toothbrush. To thoroughly clean blades, run a paper towel through the cutting process.

ENAMELWARE CASSEROLE DISHES

Fill a dish that contains stuck food bits with boiling water and 2 T. of baking soda. Let it stand and wash out.

DISHES

Save time and money by using the cheapest brand of dishwashing detergent available, but add a few tablespoons of vinegar to the dishwasher. The vinegar will cut the grease and leave your dishes sparkling clean.

Before washing fine china and crystal, place a towel on the bottom of the sink to act as a cushion.

To remove coffee or tea stains and cigarette burns from fine china, rub with a damp cloth dipped in baking soda.

DISHWASHER

Run a cup of white vinegar through the entire cycle in an empty dishwasher to remove all soap film.

CLOGGED DRAINS

When a drain is clogged with grease, pour a cup of salt and a cup of baking soda into the drain followed by a kettle of boiling water. The grease will usually dissolve immediately and open the drain.

Coffee grounds are a no-no. They do a nice job of clogging, especially if they get mixed with grease.

GARBAGE DISPOSAL

Grind a half lemon or orange rind in the disposal to remove any unpleasant odor.

OVEN

Following a spill, sprinkle with salt immediately. When oven is cool, brush off burnt food and wipe with a damp sponge.

Sprinkle bottom of oven with automatic dishwasher soap and cover with wet paper towels. Let stand for a few hours.

A quick way to clean oven parts is to place a bath towel in the bathtub and pile all removable parts from the oven onto it. Draw enough hot water to just cover the parts and sprinkle a cup of dishwasher soap over it. While you are cleaning the inside of the oven, the rest will be cleaning itself.

An inexpensive oven cleaner. Set oven on warm for about 20 minutes, then turn off. Place a small dish of full strength ammonia on the top shelf. Put large pan of boiling water on the bottom shelf and let it set overnight. In the morning, open oven and let it air a while before washing off with soap and water. Even the hard baked-on grease will wash off easily.

PLASTIC CUPS, DISHES AND CONTAINERS
Coffee or tea stains can be scoured with baking soda.

Or, fill the stained cup with hot water and drop in a few denture cleanser tablets. Let soak for 1 hour.

To rid foul odors from plastic containers, place crumbled-up newspaper (black and white only) into the container. Cover tightly and leave overnight.

REFRIGERATOR
To help eliminate odors fill a small bowl with charcoal (the kind used for potted plants) and place it on a shelf in the refrigerator. It absorbs ordors rapidly.

An open box of baking soda will absorb food odors for at least a month or two.

A little vanilla poured on a piece of cotton and place in the refrigerator will eliminate odors.

To prevent mildew from forming, wipe with vinegar. The acid effectively kills the mildew fungus.

Use a glycerine-soaked cloth to wipe sides and shelves. Future spills wipe up easily. Add after the freezer has been defrosted, coat the inside coils with glycerine. The next time you defrost, the ice will loosen quickly and drop off in sheets.

Wash inside and out with a mixture of 3 T. of baking soda in a quart of warm water.

SINKS
For a sparkling white sink, place paper towels across the bottom of your sink and saturate with household bleach. Let set for ½ hour or so.

Rub stainless steel sinks with lighter fluid if rust marks appear. After the rust disappears, wipe with your regular kitchen cleanser.

Use a cloth dampened with rubbing alcohol to remove water spots from stainless steel.

Spots on stainless steel can also be removed with white vinegar.

Club soda will shine up stainless steel sinks in a jiffy.

SPONGES
Wash in your dishwasher or soak overnight in salt water or baking soda added to water.

THERMOS BOTTLE
Fill the bottle with warm water, add 1 tsp. of baking soda and allow to soak.

TIN PIE PANS
Remove rust by dipping a raw potato in cleaning powder and scouring.

FINGERPRINTS OFF THE KITCHEN DOOR AND WALLS
Take away fingerprints and grime with a solution of half water and half ammonia. Put it in a spray bottle from one of these expensive cleaning products, you'll never have to buy them again.

FORMICA TOPS
Polish them to a sparkle with club soda.

KEEPING FOODS FRESH AND FOOD STORAGE

CELERY AND LETTUCE
Store in refrigerator in paper bags instead of plastic. Leave the outside leaves and stalks on until ready to use.

ONIONS
Once an onion has been cut in half, rub the leftover side with butter and it will keep fresh longer.

CHEESE
Wrap cheese in a vinegar-dampened cloth to keep it from drying out.

MILK
Milk at room temperature may spoil cold milk, so don't pour milk back into the carton.

BROWN SUGAR
Wrap in a plastic bag and store in refrigerator in a coffee can with a snap-on lid.

COCOA
Store cocoa in a glass jar in a dry and cool place.

CAKES
Putting half an apple in the cake box will keep cake moist.

ICE CREAM
Ice cream that has been opened and returned to the freezer sometimes forms a waxlike film on the top. To prevent this, after part of the ice cream has been removed press a piece of waxed paper against the surface and reseal the carton.

LEMONS
Store whole lemons in a tightly sealed jar of water in the refrigerator. They will yield much more juice than when first purchased.

LIMES
Store limes, wrapped in tissue paper, on lower shelf of the refrigerator.

SMOKED MEATS
Wrap ham or bacon in vinegar-soaked cloth, then in waxed paper to preserve freshness.

STRAWBERRIES
Keep in a colander in the refrigerator. Wash just before serving.

Since you have enjoyed this book, perhaps you would be interested in some of these others from QUIXOTE PRESS.

ARKANSAS BOOKS
HOW TO TALK ARKANSAS
by Bruce Carlson .... paperback $7.95
ARKANSAS' ROADKILL COOKBOOK
by Bruce Carlson .... paperback $7.95
REVENGE OF ROADKILL
by Bruce Carlson .... paperback $7.95
GHOSTS OF THE OZARKS
by Bruce Carlson .... paperback $9.95
A FIELD GUIDE TO SMALL ARKANSAS FEMALES
by Bruce Carlson .... paperback $9.95
LET'S US GO DOWN TO THE RIVER 'N...
by various authors .... paperback $9.95
ARKANSAS' VANISHING OUTHOUSE
by Bruce Carlson .... paperback $9.95
TALL TALES OF THE MISSISSIPPI RIVER
by Dan Titus .... paperback $9.95
LOST & BURIED TREASURE OF THE MISSISSIPPI RIVER
by Netha Bell & Gary Scholl .... paperback $9.95
TALES OF HACKETT'S CREEK
by Dan Titus .... paperback $9.95
UNSOLVED MYSTERIES OF THE MISSISSIPPI RIVER
by Netha Bell .... paperback $9.95
101 WAYS TO USE A DEAD RIVER FLY
by Bruce Carlson .... paperback $7.95
VACANT LOT, SCHOOL YARD & BACK ALLEY GAMES
by various authors .... paperback $9.95
HOW TO TALK MIDWESTERN
by Robert Thomas .... paperback $7.95
ARKANSAS COOKIN'
by Bruce Carlson .... (3x5) paperback $5.95

DAKOTA BOOKS

HOW TO TALK DAKOTA .... paperback $7.95
Some Pretty Tame, but Kinda Funny Stories About Early
DAKOTA LADIES-OF-THE-EVENING
by Bruce Carlson .... paperback $9.95

SOUTH DAKOTA ROADKILL COOKBOOK
by Bruce Carlson .... paperback $7.95
REVENGE OF ROADKILL
by Bruce Carlson .... paperback $7.95
101 WAYS TO USE A DEAD RIVER FLY
by Bruce Carlson .... paperback $7.95
LET'S US GO DOWN TO THE RIVER 'N...
by various authors .... paperback $9.95
LOST & BURIED TREASURE OF THE MISSOURI RIVER
by Netha Bell .... paperback $9.95
MAKIN' DO IN SOUTH DAKOTA
by various authors .... paperback $9.95
GUNSHOOTIN', WHISKEY DRINKIN', GIRL CHASIN' STORIES
OUT OF THE OLD DAKOTAS
by Netha Bell .... paperback $9.95
THE DAKOTAS' VANISHING OUTHOUSE
by Bruce Carlson .... paperback $9.95
VACANT LOT, SCHOOL YARD & BACK ALLEY GAMES
by various authors .... paperback $9.95
HOW TO TALK MIDWESTERN
by Robert Thomas .... paperback $7.95
DAKOTA COOKIN'
by Bruce Carlson .... (3x5) paperback $5.95

ILLINOIS BOOKS

ILLINOIS COOKIN'
by Bruce Carlson .... (3x5) paperback $5.95
THE VANISHING OUTHOUSE OF ILLINOIS
by Bruce Carlson .... paperback $9.95
A FIELD GUIDE TO ILLINOIS' CRITTERS
by Bruce Carlson .... paperback $7.95
YOU KNOW YOU'RE IN ILLINOIS WHEN...
by Bruce Carlson .... paperback $7.95
Some Pretty Tame, but Kinda Funny Stories About Early
ILLINOIS LADIES-OF-THE-EVENING
by Bruce Carlson .... paperback $9.95
ILLINOIS' ROADKILL COOKBOOK
by Bruce Carlson .... paperback $7.95
101 WAYS TO USE A DEAD RIVER FLY
by Bruce Carlson .... paperback $7.95

HOW TO TALK ILLINOIS
by Netha Bell .... paperback $7.95
TALL TALES OF THE MISSISSIPPI RIVER
by Dan Titus .... paperback $9.95
TALES OF HACKETT'S CREEK
by Dan Titus .... paperback $9.95
UNSOLVED MYSTERIES OF THE MISSISSIPPI
by Netha Bell .... paperback $9.95
LOST & BURIED TREASURE OF THE MISSISSIPPI RIVER
by Netha Bell & Gary Scholl .... paperback $9.95
STRANGE FOLKS ALONG THE MISSISSIPPI
by Pat Wallace .... paperback $9.95
LET'S US GO DOWN TO THE RIVER 'N...
by various authors .... paperback $9.95
MISSISSIPPI RIVER PO' FOLK
by Pat Wallace .... paperback $9.95
GHOSTS OF THE MISSISSIPPI RIVER (from Keokuk to St. Louis)
by Bruce Carlson .... paperback $9.95
GHOSTS OF THE MISSISSIPPI RIVER (from Dubuque to Keokuk)
by Bruce Carlson .... paperback $9.95
MAKIN' DO IN ILLINOIS
by various authors .... paperback $9.95
MY VERY FIRST
by various authors .... paperback $9.95
VACANT LOT, SCHOOL YARD & BACK ALLEY GAMES
by various authors .... paperback $9.95
HOW TO TALK MIDWESTERN
by Robert Thomas .... paperback $7.95

INDIANA BOOKS

HOW TO TALK INDIANA .... paperback $7.95
INDIANA'S ROADKILL COOKBOOK
by Bruce Carlson .... paperback $7.95
REVENGE OF ROADKILL
by Bruce Carlson .... paperback $7.95
A FIELD GUIDE TO SMALL INDIANA FEMALES
by Bruce Carlson .... paperback $9.95
GHOSTS OF THE OHIO RIVER (from Cincinnati to Louisville)
by Bruce Carlson .... paperback $9.95
LET'S US GO DOWN TO THE RIVER 'N...
by various authors .... paperback $9.95

101 WAYS TO USE A DEAD RIVER FLY
by Bruce Carlson .... paperback $7.95
INDIANA'S VARNISHING OUTHOUSE
by Bruce Carlson .... paperback $9.95
VACANT LOT, SCHOOL YARD & BACK ALLEY GAMES
by various authors .... paperback $9.95
HOW TO TALK MIDWESTERN
by Robert Thomas .... paperback $7.95

IOWA BOOKS

IOWA COOKIN'
by Bruce Carlson .... (3x5) paperback $5.95
IOWA'S ROADKILL COOKBOOK
By Bruce Carlson .... paperback $7.95
REVENGE OF ROADKILL
by Bruce Carlson .... paperback $7.95
IOWA'S OLD SCHOOLHOUSES
by Carole Turner Johnston .... paperback $9.95
GHOSTS OF THE AMANA COLONIES
by Lori Erickson .... paperback $9.95
GHOSTS OF THE IOWA GREAT LAKES
by Bruce Carlson .... paperback $9.95
GHOSTS OF THE MISSISSIPPI RIVER (from Dubuque to Keokuk)
by Bruce Carlson .... paperback $9.95
GHOSTS OF THE MISSISSIPPI RIVER (from Minneapolis to Dubuque)
by Bruce Carlson .... paperback $9.95
GHOSTS OF POLK COUNTY, IOWA
by Tom Welch .... paperback $9.95
TALES OF HACKETT'S CREEK
by Dan Titus .... paperback $9.95
ME 'N WESLEY (stories about the homemade toys that
Iowa farm children made and played with around the turn of the century)
by Bruce Carlson .... paperback $9.95
TALL TALES OF THE MISSISSIPPI RIVER
by Dan Titus .... paperback $9.95
HOW TO TALK IOWA .... paperback $7.95
UNSOLVED MYSTERIES OF THE MISSISSIPPI
by Netha Bell .... paperback $9.95
101 WAYS TO USE A DEAD RIVER FLY
by Bruce Carlson .... paperback $7.95

LET'S US GO DOWN TO THE RIVER 'N...
by various authors .... paperback $9.95
TRICKS WE PLAYED IN IOWA
by various authors .... paperback $9.95
IOWA, THE LAND BETWEEN THE VOWELS
(farm boy stories from the early 1900s)
by Bruce Carlson .... paperback $9.95
LOST & BURIED TREASURE OF THE MISSISSIPPI RIVER
by Netha Bell & Gary Scholl .... paperback $9.95
Some Pretty Tame, but Kinda Funny Stories About Early
IOWA LADIES-OF-THE-EVENING
by Bruce Carlson .... paperback $9.95
THE VANISHING OUTHOUSE OF IOWA
by Bruce Carlson .... paperback $9.95
IOWA'S EARLY HOME REMEDIES
by 26 students at Wapello Elem. School .... paperback $9.95
IOWA - A JOURNEY IN A PROMISED LAND
by Kathy Yoder .... paperback $16.95
LOST & BURIED TREASURE OF THE MISSOURI RIVER
by Netha Bell .... paperback $9.95
FIELD GUIDE TO IOWA'S CRITTERS
by Bruce Carlson .... paperback $7.95
OLD IOWA HOUSES, YOUNG LOVES
by Bruce Carlson .... paperback $9.95
SKUNK RIVER ANTHOLOGY
by Gene Olson .... paperback $9.95
VACANT LOT, SCHOOL YARD & BACK ALLEY GAMES
by various authors .... paperback $9.95
HOW TO TALK MIDWESTERN
by Robert Thomas .... paperback $7.95

KANSAS BOOKS

HOW TO TALK KANSAS .... paperback $7.95
STOPOVER IN KANSAS
by Jon McAlpin .... paperback $9.95
LET'S US GO DOWN TO THE RIVER 'N ...
by various authors .... paperback $9.95
LOST & BURIED TREASURE OF THE MISSOURI RIVER
by Netha Bell .... paperback $9.95

101 WAYS TO USE A DEAD RIVER FLY
by Bruce Carlson .... paperback $7.95
VACANT LOT, SCHOOL YARD & BACK ALLEY GAMES
by various authors .... paperback $9.95
HOW TO TALK MIDWESTERN
by Robert Thomas .... paperback $7.95

KENTUCKY BOOKS

GHOSTS OF THE OHIO RIVER (from Pittsburgh to Cincinnati)
by Bruce Carlson .... paperback $9.95
GHOSTS OF THE OHIO RIVER (from Cincinnati to Louisville)
by Bruce Carlson .... paperback $9.95
TALES OF HACKETT'S CREEK
by Dan Titus .... paperback $9.95
LOST & BURIED TREASURE OF THE MISSISSIPPI RIVER
by Netha Bell & Gary Scholl .... paperback $9.95
LET'S US GO DOWN TO THE RIVER 'N ...
by various authors .... paperback $9.95
UNSOLVED MYSTERIES OF THE MISSISSIPPI
by Netha Bell .... paperback $9.95
101 WAYS TO USE A DEAD RIVER FLY
by Bruce Carlson .... paperback $7.95
TALL TALES OF THE MISSISSIPPI RIVER
by Dan Titus .... paperback $9.95
MY VERY FIRST
by various authors .... paperback $9.95
VACANT LOT, SCHOOL YARD & BACK ALLEY GAMES
by various authors .... paperback $9.95

MICHIGAN BOOKS

MICHIGAN COOKIN'
by Bruce Carlson .... (3x5) paperback $5.95
MICHIGAN'S ROADKILL COOKBOOK
by Bruce Carlson .... paperback $7.95
MICHIGAN'S VANISHING OUTHOUSE
by Bruce Carlson .... paperback $9.95

MINNESOTA BOOKS

MINNESOTA'S ROADKILL COOKBOOK
    by Bruce Carlson .... paperback $7.95
REVENGE OF ROADKILL
    by Bruce Carlson .... paperback $7.95
A FIELD GUIDE TO SMALL MINNESOTA FEMALES
    by Bruce Carlson .... paperback $9.95
GHOSTS OF THE MISSISSIPPI RIVER (from Minneapolis to Dubuque)
    by Bruce Carlson .... paperback $9.95
LAKES COUNTRY COOKBOOK
    by Bruce Carlson .... paperback $11.95
UNSOLVED MYSTERIES OF THE MISSISSIPPI
    by Netha Bell .... paperback $9.95
TALES OF HACKETT'S CREEK
    by Dan Titus .... paperback $9.95
GHOSTS OF SOUTHWEST MINNESOTA
    by Ruth Hein .... paperback $9.95
HOW TO TALK LIKE A MINNESOTA NATIVE .... paperback $7.95
MINNESOTA'S VANISHING OUTHOUSE
    by Bruce Carlson .... paperback $9.95
TALL TALES OF THE MISSISSIPPI RIVER
    by Dan Titus .... paperback $9.95
Some Pretty Tame, but Kinda Funny Stories About Early
MINNESOTA LADIES-OF-THE-EVENING
    by Bruce Carlson .... paperback $9.95
101 WAYS TO USE A DEAD RIVER FLY .... paperback $7.95
LOST & BURIED TREASURE OF THE MISSISSIPPI RIVER
    by Netha Bell & Gary Scholl .... paperback $9.95
VACANT LOT, SCHOOL YARD & BACK ALLEY GAMES
    by various authors .... paperback $9.95
HOW TO TALK MIDWESTERN
    by Robert Thomas .... paperback $7.95
MINNESOTA COOKIN'
    by Bruce Carlson .... (3x5) paperback $5.95

MISSOURI BOOKS

MISSOURI COOKIN'
    by Bruce Carlson .... (3x5) paperback $5.95
MISSOURI'S ROADKILL COOKBOOK
    by Bruce Carlson .... paperback $7.95

REVENGE OF ROADKILL
by Bruce Carlson .... paperback $7.95
LET'S US GO DOWN TO THE RIVER 'N ...
by various authors .... paperback $9.95
LAKES COUNTRY COOKBOOK
by Bruce Carlson .... paperback $11.95
101 WAYS TO USE A DEAD RIVER FLY
by Bruce Carlson .... paperback $7.95
TALL TALES OF THE MISSISSIPPI RIVER
by Dan Titus .... paperback $9.95
TALES OF HACKETT'S CREEK
by Dan Titus .... paperback $9.95
STRANGE FOLKS ALONG THE MISSISSIPPI
by Pat Wallace .... paperback $9.95
LOST & BURIED TREASURE OF THE MISSOURI RIVER
by Netha Bell .... paperback $9.95
HOW TO TALK MISSOURIAN
by Bruce Carlson .... paperback $7.95
VACANT LOT, SCHOOL YARD & BACK ALLEY GAMES
by various authors .... paperback $9.95
HOW TO TALK MIDWESTERN
by Robert Thomas .... paperback $7.95
UNSOLVED MYSTERIES OF THE MISSISSIPPI
by Netha Bell .... paperback $9.95
LOST & BURIED TREASURE OF THE MISSISSIPPI RIVER
by Netha Bell & Gary Scholl .... paperback $9.95
MISSISSIPPI RIVER PO' FOLK
by Pat Wallace .... paperback $9.95
Some Pretty Tame, but Kinda Funny Stories About Early
MISSOURI LADIES-OF-THE-EVENING
by Bruce Carlson .... paperback $9.95
GUNSHOOTIN', WHISKEY DRINKIN', GIRL CHASIN'
STORIES OUT OF THE OLD MISSOURI TERRITORY
by Bruce Carlson .... paperback $9.95
THE VANISHING OUTHOUSE OF MISSOURI
by Bruce Carlson .... paperback $9.95
A FIELD GUIDE TO MISSOURI'S CRITTERS
by Bruce Carlson .... paperback $7.95
EARLY MISSOURI HOME REMEDIES
by various authors .... paperback $9.95
GHOSTS OF THE OZARKS
by Bruce Carlson .... paperback $9.95

MISSISSIPPI RIVER COOKIN' BOOK
by Bruce Carlson .... paperback $11.95
MISSOURI'S OLD HOUSES, AND NEW LOVES
by Bruce Carlson .... paperback $9.95
UNDERGROUND MISSOURI
by Bruce Carlson .... paperback $9.95

NEBRASKA BOOKS

LOST & BURIED TREASURE OF THE MISSOURI RIVER
by Netha Bell .... paperback $9.95
101 WAYS TO USE A DEAD RIVER FLY
by Bruce Carlson .... paperback $7.95
LET'S US GO DOWN TO THE RIVER 'N ...
by various authors .... paperback $9.95
HOW TO TALK MIDWESTERN
by Robert Thomas .... paperback $7.95
VACANT LOT, SCHOOL YARD & BACK ALLEY GAMES
by various authors .... paperback $9.95

TENNESSEE BOOKS

TALES OF HACKETT'S CREED
by Dan Titus .... paperback $9.95
TALL TALES OF THE MISSISSIPPI RIVER
by Dan Titus .... paperback $9.95
UNSOLVED MYSTERIES OF THE MISSISSIPPI
by Netha Bell .... paperback $9.95
LOST & BURIED TREASURE OF THE MISSISSIPPI RIVER
by Netha Bell & Gary Scholl .... paperback $9.95
LET'S US GO DOWN TO THE RIVER 'N ...
by various authors .... paperback $9.95
101 WAYS TO USE A DEAD RIVER FLY
by Bruce Carlson .... paperback $7.95
VACANT LOT, SCHOOL YARD & BACK ALLEY GAMES
by various authors .... paperback $9.95

WISCONSIN BOOKS

HOW TO TALK WISCONSIN .... paperback $7.95
WISCONSIN COOKIN'
    by Bruce Carlson .... (3x5) paperback $5.95
WISCONSIN'S ROADKILL COOKBOOK
    by Bruce Carlson .... paperback $7.95
REVENGE OF ROADKILL
    by Bruce Carlson .... paperback $7.95
TALL TALES OF THE MISSISSIPPI RIVER
    by Dan Titus .... paperback $9.95
LAKES COUNTRY COOKBOOK
    by Bruce Carlson .... paperback $11.95
TALES OF HACKETT'S CREEK
    by Dan Titus .... paperback $9.95
LET'S US GO DOWN TO THE RIVER 'N ...
    by various authors .... paperback $9.95
101 WAYS TO USE A DEAD RIVER FLY
    by Bruce Carlson .... paperback $7.95
UNSOLVED MYSTERIES OF THE MISSISSIPPI
    by Netha Bell .... paperback $9.95
LOST & BURIED TREASURE OF THE MISSISSIPPI RIVER
    by Netha Bell & Gary Scholl .... paperback $9.95
GHOSTS OF THE MISSISSIPPI RIVER (from Dubuque to Keokuk)
    by Bruce Carlson .... paperback $9.95
HOW TO TALK MIDWESTERN
    by Robert Thomas .... paperback $7.95
VACANT LOT, SCHOOL YARD & BACK ALLEY GAMES
    by various authors .... paperback $9.95
MY VERY FIRST
    by various authors .... paperback $9.95
EARLY WISCONSIN HOME REMEDIES
    by various authors .... paperback $9.95
GHOSTS OF THE MISSISSIPPI RIVER (from Minneapolis to Dubuque)
    by Bruce Carlson .... paperback $9.95
THE VANISHING OUTHOUSE OF WISCONSIN
    by Bruce Carlson .... paperback $9.95
GHOSTS OF DOOR COUNTY, WISCONSIN
    by Geri Rider .... paperback $9.95
Some Pretty Tame, but Kinda Funny Stories About Early
WISCONSIN LADIES-OF-THE-EVENING
    by Bruce Carlson .... paperback $9.95

MIDWESTERN BOOKS

A FIELD GUIDE TO THE MIDWEST'S WORST RESTAURANTS
by Bruce Carlson .... paperback $5.95
THE MOTORIST'S FIELD GUIDE TO MIDWESTERN FARM
EQUIPMENT (misguided information as only a city slicker can give it)
by Bruce Carlson .... paperback $5.95
VACANT LOT, SCHOOL YARD & BACK ALLEY GAMES
OF THE MIDWEST YEARS AGO
by various authors .... paperback $9.95
MIDWEST SMALL TOWN COOKING
by Bruce Carlson .... (3x5) paperback $5.95
HITCHHIKING THE UPPER MIDWEST
by Bruce Carlson .... paperback $7.95
101 WAYS FOR MIDWESTERNERS TO "DO IN" THEIR
NEIGHBOR'S PESKY DOG WITHOUT GETTING CAUGHT
by Bruce Carlson .... paperback $5.95

RIVER BOOKS

ON THE SHOULDERS OF A GIANT
by M. Cody and D. Walker .... paperback $9.95
SKUNK RIVER ANTHOLOGY
by Gene "Will" Olson .... paperback $9.95
JACK KING vs. DETECTIVE MACKENZIE
by Netha Bell .... paperback $9.95
LOST & BURIED TREASURES ALONG THE MISSISSIPPI
by Netha Bell & Gary Scholl .... paperback $9.95
MISSISSIPPI RIVER PO' FOLK
by Pat Wallace .... paperback $9.95
STRANGE FOLKS ALONG THE MISSISSIPPI
by Pat Wallace .... paperback $9.95
GHOSTS OF THE OHIO RIVER (from Pittsburgh to Cincinnati)
by Bruce Carlson .... paperback $9.95
GHOSTS OF THE OHIO RIVER (from Cincinnati to Louisville)
by Bruce Carlson .... paperback $9.95
GHOSTS OF THE MISSISSIPPI RIVER (Minneapolis to Dubuque)
by Bruce Carlson .... paperback $9.95
GHOSTS OF THE MISSISSIPPI RIVER (Dubuque to Keokuk)
by Bruce Carlson .... paperback $9.95
TALL TALES OF THE MISSISSIPPI RIVER
by Dan Titus .... paperback $9.95

TALL TALES OF THE MISSOURI RIVER
by Dan Titus .... paperback $9.95
RIVER SHARKS & SHENANIGANS
(tales of riverboat gambling of years ago)
by Netha Bell .... paperback $9.95
UNSOLVED MYSTERIES OF THE MISSISSIPPI
by Netha Bell .... paperback $9.95
TALES OF HACKETT'S CREEK (1940s Mississippi River kids)
by Dan Titus .... paperback $9.95
101 WAYS TO USE A DEAD RIVER FLY
by Bruce Carlson .... paperback $7.95
LET'S US GO DOWN TO THE RIVER 'N ...
by various authors .... paperback $9.95
LOST & BURIED TREASURE OF THE MISSOURI
by Netha Bell .... paperback $9.95

COOKBOOKS

ROARING 20's COOKBOOK
by Bruce Carlson .... paperback $11.95
DEPRESSION COOKBOOK
by Bruce Carlson .... paperback $11.95
LAKES COUNTRY COOKBOOK
by Bruce Carlson .... paperback $11.95
A COOKBOOK FOR THEM WHAT AIN'T DONE A LOT OF COOKIN'
by Bruce Carlson .... paperback $11.95
FLAT-OUT DIRT-CHEAP COOKIN' COOKBOOK
by Bruce Carlson .... paperback $11.95
APHRODISIAC COOKING
by Bruce Carlson .... paperback $11.95
WILD CRITTER COOKBOOK
by Bruce Carlson .... paperback $11.95
I GOT FUNNIER-THINGS-TO-DO-THAN-COOKIN' COOKBOOK
by Louise Lum .... paperback $11.95
MISSISSIPPI RIVER COOKIN' BOOK
by Bruce Carlson .... paperback $11.95
HUNTING IN THE NUDE COOKBOOK
by Bruce Carlson .... paperback $9.95
DAKOTA COOKIN'
by Bruce Carlson .... (3x5) paperback $5.95
IOWA COOKIN'
by Bruce Carlson .... (3x5) paperback $5.95

MICHIGAN COOKIN'
  by Bruce Carlson .... (3x5) paperback $5.95
MINNESOTA COOKIN'
  by Bruce Carlson .... (3x5) paperback $5.95
MISSOURI COOKIN'
  by Bruce Carlson .... (3x5) paperback $5.95
ILLINOIS COOKIN'
  by Bruce Carlson .... (3x5) paperback $5.95
WISCONSIN COOKIN'
  by Bruce Carlson .... (3x5) paperback $5.95
HILL COUNTRY COOKIN'
  by Bruce Carlson .... (3x5) paperback $5.95
MIDWEST SMALL TOWN COOKIN'
  by Bruce Carlson .... (3x5) paperback $5.95
APHRODISIAC COOKIN'
  by Bruce Carlson .... (3x5) paperback $5.95
PREGNANT LADY COOKIN'
  by Bruce Carlson .... (3x5) paperback $5.95
GOOD COOKIN' FROM THE PLAIN PEOPLE
  by Bruce Carlson .... (3x5) paperback $5.95
WORKING GIRL COOKING
  by Bruce Carlson .... (3x5) paperback $5.95
COOKING FOR ONE
  by Barb Layton .... paperback $11.95
SUPER SIMPLE COOKING
  by Barb Layton .... (3x5) paperback $5.95
OFF TO COLLEGE COOKBOOK
  by Barb Layton .... (3x5) paperback $5.95
COOKING WITH THINGS THAT GO SPLASH
  by Bruce Carlson .... (3x5) paperback $5.95
COOKING WITH THINGS THAT GO MOO
  by Bruce Carlson .... (3x5) paperback $5.95
COOKING WITH SPIRITS
  by Bruce Carlson .... (3x5) paperback $5.95
INDIAN COOKING COOKBOOK
  by Bruce Carlson .... paperback $9.95
DIAL-A-DREAM COOKBOOK
  by Bruce Carlson .... (3x5) paperback $5.95
HORMONE HELPER COOKBOOK .... (3x5) paperback $5.95

MISCELLANEOUS BOOKS

DEAR TABBY (letters to and from a feline advice columnist)
by Bruce Carlson .... paperback $5.95
HOW TO BEHAVE (etiquette advice for non-traditional
and awkward circumstances such as attending dogfights,
what to do when your blind date turns out to be your spouse, etc.)
by Bruce Carlson .... paperback $5.95
REVENGE OF THE ROADKILL
by Bruce Carlson .... paperback $7.95

Write Your Own Recipes Here

Write Your Own Recipes Here

Write Your Own Recipes Here

Write Your Own Recipes Here